Cambridge Elements

Elements in Political Philosophy
edited by
Cécile Laborde
University of Oxford
Steven Wall
University of Arizona

WRONGFUL DISCRIMINATION

Kasper Lippert-Rasmussen
Centre for the Experimental-Philosophical Study of Discrimination, University of Aarhus

Shaftesbury Road, Cambridge CB2 8EA, United Kingdom

One Liberty Plaza, 20th Floor, New York, NY 10006, USA

477 Williamstown Road, Port Melbourne, VIC 3207, Australia

314–321, 3rd Floor, Plot 3, Splendor Forum, Jasola District Centre, New Delhi – 110025, India

103 Penang Road, #05–06/07, Visioncrest Commercial, Singapore 238467

Cambridge University Press is part of Cambridge University Press & Assessment, a department of the University of Cambridge.

We share the University's mission to contribute to society through the pursuit of education, learning and research at the highest international levels of excellence.

www.cambridge.org
Information on this title: www.cambridge.org/9781009596725

DOI: 10.1017/9781009596749

© Kasper Lippert-Rasmussen 2025

This publication is in copyright. Subject to statutory exception and to the provisions of relevant collective licensing agreements, no reproduction of any part may take place without the written permission of Cambridge University Press & Assessment.

When citing this work, please include a reference to the DOI 10.1017/9781009596749

First published 2025

A catalogue record for this publication is available from the British Library

ISBN 978-1-009-59672-5 Hardback
ISBN 978-1-009-59675-6 Paperback
ISSN 2976-5706 (online)
ISSN 2976-5692 (print)

Cambridge University Press & Assessment has no responsibility for the persistence or accuracy of URLs for external or third-party internet websites referred to in this publication and does not guarantee that any content on such websites is, or will remain, accurate or appropriate.

For EU product safety concerns, contact us at Calle de José Abascal, 56, 1°, 28003 Madrid, Spain, or email eugpsr@cambridge.org

Wrongful Discrimination

Elements in Political Philosophy

DOI: 10.1017/9781009596749
First published online: October 2025

Kasper Lippert-Rasmussen
Centre for the Experimental-Philosophical Study of Discrimination, University of Aarhus

Author for correspondence: Kasper Lippert-Rasmussen, lippert@ps.au.dk

Abstract: In a generic sense, to discriminate is to differentiate. Generic discrimination is not wrongful. But many instances of a more specific form of discrimination – differentiating between people because they are members of different socially salient groups (henceforth: *group discrimination*) – are wrongful. This means that people subjected to group discrimination are often wronged, and this bears importantly on whether such acts are morally impermissible. The three main accounts of what makes group discrimination wrongful appeal to considerations of harm, disrespect, and social relations of inequality, respectively. While each of them can explain the wrongfulness of some paradigmatic instances of wrongful direct discrimination, they explain the wrongfulness of a set of three important non-paradigmatic forms of discrimination – indirect discrimination, implicit bias, and algorithmic discrimination – less well. Overall, the prospects of a monistic account of the wrongfulness of discrimination are bleak.

Keywords: algorithmic discrimination, discrimination, harm, implicit bias, indirect discrimination, relational equality, respect

© Kasper Lippert-Rasmussen 2025

ISBNs: 9781009596725 (HB), 9781009596756 (PB), 9781009596749 (OC)
ISSNs: 2976-5706 (online), 2976-5692 (print)

Contents

1 Discrimination and Wrongful Discrimination 1

2 Harm 14

3 Disrespect 22

4 Social Equality 31

5 Indirect Discrimination 38

6 Implicit Bias Discrimination 48

7 Algorithmic Discrimination 55

8 Conclusion 67

References 68

1 Discrimination and Wrongful Discrimination

1.1 Introduction

United Kingdom citizens' voting rights do not depend on gender. However, only in 1928 did UK women acquire the right to vote. In 1866, John Stuart Mill proposed an amendment to the House of Commons extending voting rights to women. Along with many similar ones in the years to come, this proposal was defeated by a large margin. Today, most would consider male-only voting rights an egregious example of wrongful gender discrimination. However, in his *The Subjection of Women* (1869), Mill never used the term 'discrimination' to refer to the many practices, including male-only voting rights, that he opposed in the spirit of gender equality. Nor was the term often employed by the civil rights activists who opposed Jim Crow laws targeting Blacks in the United States prior to 1964. Martin Luther King used the term only once in his August 1963 'I Have a Dream' speech.

Presently, 'discrimination' is used to label a wide range of wrongful practices. It is used to cover forms of gender or race discrimination that are less egregious than male-only voting rights and racist Jim Crow laws – for example, microaggressions. The term is also used to pick out disadvantageous treatment of groups that were largely ignored when complaints about race and gender discrimination became more common in the 1960s – for example, disabled people, LGBTQ+ people, and people who are unattractive according to conventional standards of beauty. Considering this striking linguistic development, one might ask: what is discrimination?

1.2 Senses of Discrimination

According to dictionaries, 'to discriminate' is to differentiate. Anyone engages in discrimination *in this generic sense* all the time – for example, we treat friends differently from strangers. Hence, what people who object to discrimination dislike is a specific form of differentiation. What is it? Four suggestions spring to mind.

First, on one view, discrimination in the relevant specific sense is morally wrongful differentiation (henceforth: *moralised discrimination*). If something is not morally wrongful, then by definition it is not discrimination. An advantage of this notion is that, unlike generic discrimination, we should clearly be concerned about discrimination in this sense. However, its usefulness is limited by the fact that sometimes people agree that something is discrimination and yet disagree about whether it is wrongful. A policy of giving priority to younger over older patients when doctors cannot save the lives of all is age discrimination, and not just in the generic sense. Yet people disagree about whether it is morally wrongful. Arguably, this could be described as a disagreement about whether age discrimination in a healthcare setting is morally wrongful. Also, on the moralised definition, 'Because it is discrimination' is as uninformative an answer to the question 'Why is it wrongful?' as 'Because he is a bachelor' is to 'Why is he unmarried?' Neither answer supplies any new information to a competent language user. However, the former answer to 'Why is it wrongful?' is informative in many contexts (see also Section 5.4 on a moralised notion of proportionality).

Second, another view holds that discrimination in the relevant specific sense is differentiation based on irrelevant traits (henceforth: *irrelevance discrimination*). An advantage of this notion is that, plausibly, paradigmatic cases of job market discrimination involve hiring based on irrelevant traits – for example, gender – rather than hiring based on relevant properties – for example, qualifications. However, to adequately grasp the notion of irrelevance discrimination, we need to understand when traits are relevant. If a trait is relevant if, and only if, it is such that it is not morally wrongful to differentiate based on whether a person has this trait, then irrelevance discrimination collapses into moralised discrimination.

People who employ the notion of irrelevance discrimination have a different understanding of relevance. They think that, for many activities, one can identify certain aims that are morally permissible. Traits that bear on whether an agent who engages in that activity is better or worse at achieving these aims are relevant. For example, a morally permissible aim of running a business is making a profit. Accordingly, a trait that bears on the business owner's prospects of making a profit is relevant. This is one reason why women are discriminated against when their applications are not assessed based on their ability to contribute to the employer's profits. Nevertheless, irrelevance discrimination is not the most fruitful notion of discrimination in the present context. Sometimes gender or race *are* relevant traits in the indicated sense – for example, when customers are sexist and accordingly the gender of employees might make a difference to profits. Employers responsive to such differences discriminate in the sense that people who worry about discrimination have in mind and yet do not engage in irrelevance discrimination. Moreover, it is possible to differentiate between people on irrelevant grounds without doing anything wrongful akin to what people have in mind when they think about wrongful discrimination. An employer who idiosyncratically refuses to hire any person who is a Tottenham Hotspur fan treats such applicants unfairly. But, arguably, the moral problem which employers such as this one pose is different from the moral problem of discrimination on the job market that systemically targets specific groups.

Third, a common view is that discrimination in the relevant specific sense is differentiation that disadvantages legally protected groups (henceforth: *illegal discrimination*). One advantage of this suggestion is that in many cases where people object to what they see as morally wrongful discrimination, these cases involve disadvantageous treatment of members of legally protected groups. The flip side of this advantage is that there is nothing that prevents a law's list of protected groups from being morally deficient. As my two opening examples indicate, we do not have to go far back in UK or US history before we can find compelling examples of wrongful discrimination against groups that then were the opposite of legally protected groups.

Lastly, a final view of the relevant specific form of discrimination – the one that I will employ in the rest of this Element – is that discrimination is differentiation based on membership in socially salient groups (henceforth: *group discrimination*). A socially salient group is one which is such that perceived membership in it makes a significant difference to a wide range of different social interactions. Race, gender, religion, and sexual orientation are traits that sort people into different socially salient groups, while whether one has green or blue eyes is not, and that is an important attraction of the concept of group discrimination. Sexual orientation is tricky in the sense that we are often not aware of the sexual orientation of people with whom we interact – for example, in homophobic societies, LGBTQ+ people hide their sexuality in many contexts. However, *if* they were to be perceived as LGBTQ+ in such contexts, that would make a significant difference to social interactions (cf. Singh and Wodak 2023).

Group discrimination has the virtues of the three other more specific notions of discrimination while avoiding their vices. Like moralised discrimination, group discrimination is tied to a concern for moral wrongfulness because of the contingent but relatively reliable connection between acting wrongfully and treating people based on their membership in socially salient groups. Moreover, the notion of group discrimination permits us to describe the debate about young versus old patients referred to earlier in this section as one where the parties disagree about the wrongfulness of age discrimination in a healthcare context. Like irrelevance discrimination, it classifies paradigmatic cases of job market discrimination as such, but it avoids the tricky issue of which qualifications are relevant and allows us to classify as discriminatory cases where applicants' gender amounts to relevant, so-called reaction qualifications (as in a case where customers are sexist), even if applicants are treated only based on relevant properties. Cases of idiosyncratic differential treatment – recall the example of the employer who dislikes Tottenham Hotspur fans – which generally are not regarded as cases of discrimination do not fall under the extension of group discrimination. And, finally, many socially salient groups are protected groups in many countries, and yet group discrimination allows us to classify intuitive instances of discrimination as such even if the discriminatees do not enjoy any special legal status (Lippert-Rasmussen 2013, 14–36).

That said, some theorists explicitly deny that socially salient group membership forms the only basis on which one can suffer discrimination. Some deny this because they think idiosyncratic disadvantageous treatment involves the same moral wrong as group discrimination – for example, failing to take the victim's personhood into account (Eidelson 2015; see also Mason 2023; Thomsen 2013). Moreover, a few instances of differential treatment are based on facts other than membership of socially salient groups that are generally considered discrimination – most prominently so-called genetic discrimination where, say, people are charged different insurance premiums based on genetic tests used to predict their risk of developing certain diseases. There are many groups that seem neither socially salient, nor socially non-salient – for example, smokers. However, since it is often highly debated whether members of such groups are discriminated against when they are being treated disadvantageously, the wider debate attests to the influence of the centrality of the idea of group discrimination.

Inspired by an influential article (and later work) by Kimberlé Crenshaw (1989), many theorists think that intersectionality is an important feature of discrimination, and some might think that this speaks against the notion of group discrimination. In that work, Crenshaw discusses a legal case against General Motors, where a complaint on behalf of Black women was rejected based on the fact that a disproportionately large proportion of workers laid off came from this group on the ground that it was neither the case that a disproportionately large number of Black workers had been laid off, nor the case that a disproportionately large number of female workers had been laid off. This sort of reasoning, Crenshaw argues, is blind to the experiences of Black women at the intersection of race and gender discrimination, because, unlike Blacks and unlike women, Black women do not constitute a legally protected category. In my view, Crenshaw's argument is convincing, but it does not clash with the notion of group discrimination because groups can be socially salient even if they do not form legally protected categories.

1.3 Types of Group Discrimination

There are different subspecies of group discrimination, and these might be wrongful in different ways. For this reason, this subsection introduces a bit of taxonomy over different kinds of group discrimination. The most important distinction is the one between direct and indirect discrimination, or, as it is often put in a US context, disparate treatment and disparate impact (Altman 2020). This distinction is drawn in different ways by different theorists. For present purposes, I adopt the following definitions:

> The discriminator directly discriminates against the discriminatee relative to a comparator (i.e., one whose treatment by the discriminator forms a relevant comparison to the discriminator's treatment of the discriminatee) if, and only if:
>
> (1) the discriminator treats the discriminatee disadvantageously relative to the comparator;
> (2) (1) is true because the discriminator represents the discriminatee and not the comparator as having a certain trait;
> (3) and that trait is membership in a socially salient group (cf. Shelby 2007, 131).

Direct discrimination contrasts with indirect discrimination:

> The discriminator indirectly discriminates against the discriminatee relative to the comparator if, and only if:
>
> (4) the discriminator treats the discriminatee and the comparator in the same way;
> (5) treating the discriminatee and the comparator in this way disadvantages people like the discriminatee relative to people like the comparator;
> (6) and the disadvantages imposed on people like the discriminatee are disproportionate relative to the benefits involved in treating the discriminator and the comparator and people like them in the relevant way (cf. Moreau 2020, 17).

By way of illustration, suppose a university's recruitment policies are gender-neutral and are applied gender neutrally – that is, (4) is satisfied. One important criterion is number of publications, and it so happens that because the burden of childbirth and childcare disproportionately falls on women, female applicants for tenured position typically on average have fewer publications than male applicants. Hence, the use of this criterion disadvantages female applicants who apply for a permanent position – that is, (5) is satisfied. And, finally, this disadvantage is disproportionate, say, because female academics tend to outperform, productivity-wise, male academics in those later stages of an academic's career when, typically, academics no longer have small children – that is, (6) is satisfied.

Direct discrimination concerns how the discriminator responds to the discriminatee qua member of a particular socially salient group, whereas indirect discrimination is about the consequences of the discriminator's actions (Campbell and Smith 2023, 319; cf. Cosette-Lefebvre 2020; Fredman 2018).

But let us further unpack the conditions in the definitions of the two species of discrimination, the latter of which we will discuss in greater detail in Section 5.

Direct discrimination, unlike indirect discrimination, involves unequal, disadvantageous treatment ((1) and (4)). What it is to treat people in the same way is a tricky question, but if, say, employers apply the same, facially neutral criteria of promotion irrespective of the race of the candidate, this will be considered equal treatment even if racial minority candidates are less likely to meet the criteria, provided the criteria in question are not adopted with the intention of disadvantaging racial minority candidates. However, there are cases of applying the same, facially neutral rules to everyone which, intuitively and whatever the underlying intention, are not cases of treating people equally – for example, a rule saying that whatever their gender, no one is allowed to breastfeed their baby on the job.

What it is to 'treat' someone is also tricky, but generally discrimination theorists have in mind conduct that has relatively concrete effects on the discriminatee. I do not treat people differently by allowing myself to daydream about doing nice things to some people and bad things to others. Because it is impossible both to treat some disadvantageously relatively to others while at the same time treating them in the same way, (1) and (4) imply that an instance of discrimination cannot be an instance of both direct and indirect discrimination.

Conditions (2) and (3) together imply that the discriminator treats the discriminatee disadvantageously because of the discriminatee's perceived membership in a socially salient group. One way in which (2) and (3) can be true is by the discriminator intending to treat the discriminatee in a way that amounts to treating this person disadvantageously. However, (2) and (3) can also be true in the complete absence of any such intention – for example, if the discriminator because of implicit bias underestimates the qualifications of female applicants and for that reason does not hire a female applicant, but also would not have hired a male applicant with the same perceived qualifications. However, not all implicit bias discrimination – for example, disadvantageous treatment rooted in non-propositionally structured patterns of association (see Section 6) – qualifies as direct discrimination.

Condition (5) indicates that the focus in indirect discrimination is on the downstream consequences of the treatment. These consequences must in some sense be negative for the treatment to amount to indirect discrimination *against*.

Finally, (6) implies that the disadvantages must be disproportionate. Something can be disproportionate only in relation to something else. The simplest view here is that this 'something else' refers to the benefits involved in the putatively indirectly discriminatory treatment for the discriminator and others (but see Section 5.3). On the face of it, disproportionality is a normative criterion – that is, it is a criterion which speaks to whether a certain set of advantages are sufficiently weighty considering the disadvantages to putative discriminatees to justify otherwise indirectly discriminatory treatment. No such disproportionality condition is part of standard definitions of direct discrimination, which is thus another crucial difference between the two. Finally, while European discrimination laws typically explicitly include a disproportionality requirement, in a US context, it is more common to require that the relevant treatment with disparate impact is unnecessary relative to the discriminator's reasonably held goals – for example, because there is an alternative treatment that has less disparate impact and serves the discriminator's goals no less well. Nevertheless, I shall persist in referring to disproportionality in part because, on a plausible interpretation, the standard US necessity condition amounts to a particular demanding version of the disproportionality condition – that is, to the effect that impact of a treatment is disproportionate only if alternative treatments involve no costs for the employer in terms of reasonable goal achievement.

There are other important distinctions between different kinds of discrimination. One is the distinction between statistical and non-statistical discrimination. Statistical discrimination is discrimination that, in addition to (1) and (3), satisfies:

> Condition (2*) (1) is true because the discriminator represents the discriminatee and not the comparator as having a certain proxy trait – for example, a certain racial identity – and because the discriminator takes having this proxy trait, to which the discriminator is indifferent as such, to be statistically correlated with a target trait which the discriminator cares about – for example, being involved in crime.

Non-statistical discrimination is discrimination that does not satisfy (1), (2*), and (3). Condition (2*) can be true in either of two ways. First, the discriminator might more often stop and frisk men because the discriminator believes men are more likely to be involved in crime than women. Second, the discriminator might more often stop and frisk men than women because the discriminator believes that gender is correlated with crime but has no beliefs about which gender is positively correlated with crime – for example, the discriminator simply feeds a computer information about any given target person's gender, among other things, and then acts on the computer's recommendation about whom to stop and frisk. In the first case, we have direct statistical discrimination against men. In the second case, we have indirect statistical discrimination against men. As this slightly contrived illustration indicates, such cases are possible, but probably rare (Lippert-Rasmussen 2013, 87–89).

A target property being statistically correlated with a target trait does not imply that having the proxy makes it highly likely that the discriminatee has the target trait. It suffices that it is more likely that the discriminatee has the target trait if they have the proxy trait than if they do not have it. We will address an arguably special form of statistical discrimination – algorithmic discrimination – more closely in Section 7.

Finally, it is common for both laypeople and theorists to refer to structural discrimination, thus implicitly positing such a thing as non-structural discrimination. In connection with the Black Lives Matter movement, it is often said that the problem is not 'rotten apples', but structural racism in the police force. While there are few attempts at offering a precise definition of structural discrimination, typically the motivation for introducing the notion of structural discrimination is to point to the fact that even if there are no agents – whether individual or collective agents – that engage in direct or indirect discrimination, social rules and practices could still result in 'discriminatory outcomes'. Hence, I propose:

> The discriminatee is subjected to structural discrimination relative to the comparator if, and only if:
>
> (7) the discriminatee is disadvantaged relative to the comparator;
> (8) where (7) is a result of certain social structures;
> (9) these social structures are a result of or constituted by many acts of past or present direct or indirect discrimination against the discriminatee relative to the comparator by many different agents;
> (10) the 'discriminatee' and the 'comparator' refer to socially salient groups; and
> (11) the disadvantages to the discriminatee are disproportional to the benefits. (Lippert-Rasmussen 2024b)

Condition (7) reflects that the definition is one of structural discrimination *against* the discriminatee. Condition (8) reflects that the discrimination is structural in a way to be specified further. Condition (9) distinguishes structural discrimination from structural injustice in general. This condition implies that structural discrimination can obtain even if no individual agent presently engages in discrimination against the disadvantaged group, provided that many agents did so in the past and that the social structure that makes the relevant social group disadvantaged results from those past acts. Condition (10) implies that the direct victims of structural discrimination are groups, not individuals. Condition (11) is included for two reasons: to render the notion of structural discrimination in one respect parallel to indirect discrimination, and to avoid that virtually any disadvantage to a socially salient group caused by social structures amounts to structural discrimination.

On this definition, structural discrimination is quite different from direct and indirect discrimination. First, structural discrimination is a patterned disparity with a particular kind of explanation. The property of being structurally discriminatory is not a property of an individual agent's actions. However, as (9) points to, the existence of the relevant discriminatory social structures is partly a matter of many individuals acting in directly or indirectly discriminatory ways.

Second, the distinction between structural and non-structural discrimination is orthogonal to the distinction between direct and indirect discrimination. Structural as well as non-structural discrimination might involve direct or indirect discrimination. Specifically, structural discrimination is not a particular subspecies of indirect discrimination. For any instance of direct or indirect discrimination, there is a discriminating agent of that instance of discrimination. The same is not true of structural discrimination.

Finally, those who are subjected to structural discrimination are primarily socially salient groups and only secondarily individual members of those groups, viz. (10). This is unlike direct and indirect discrimination, where the primary discriminatees are individual members of socially salient groups, and where it is possible for individual members of a social salient group to be subjected to direct or indirect discrimination without all other members being so as well. Female employees of a particular company cannot complain against structural sexism in employment if, generally, employment structures benefit women relative to men. Nevertheless, individual female employees could still be subjected to direct and indirect discrimination by their employer.

1.4 Ways in which Discrimination Can Be Wrongful

What makes group discrimination wrongful? This question seems relatively straightforward, but several complications arise. First, one lesson from Section 1.3 is that instances of discrimination can be quite different and, accordingly, that depending on the correct moral view, different instances of discrimination could be wrongful for different reasons. It might be that direct discrimination is wrongful when it is, because it is disrespectful in virtue of the discriminator's mental states. Arguably, structural discrimination cannot be wrongful for that reason, but might be so because of how it clashes with distributive justice. In short: according to monism, there is one and only one wrongful-making feature of all instances of wrongful discrimination. Pluralism holds that there are two or more such features.

Second, this Element is entitled *Wrongful Discrimination*. Its title could have been *Morally Impermissible Discrimination*. However, that would indicate a different topic. Something can be wrongful even if it is not impermissible. It might be wrongful to frame an innocent person to save the lives of hundreds, even if it is not morally impermissible, all things considered, to do so. The innocent person being framed has no duty to be framed and holds a moral complaint against us if we frame them. Hence, in using them to save the greater number, we incur obligations – for example, to apologise and compensate, even if what we did was morally permissible, all things considered. Conversely, things can be morally impermissible even if they wrong no one. It might be morally impermissible to engage in a racist embryo selection programme, even if no one is wronged, say, because (strangely) no one of the deselected race has ever existed or, because of the selection programme, ever will.

Some moral theories do not acknowledge a possible gap between wrongful and morally impermissible discrimination. Utilitarianism condemns many instances of discrimination because they fail to maximise the sum of welfare. However, the victims of the welfare-reducing discriminatory acts have no special moral standing to complain about the treatment to which they are subjected. They can complain about the fact that the discriminatory treatment they are subjected to reduces overall welfare and thus prevents bringing about the best outcome on a relevant impersonal ranking. But, according to utilitarianism, anyone, including perpetrators, can do that. If, however, discrimination can be wrongful, victims of wrongful discriminatory acts have a special standing to complain about it – for example, they might have a claim on their discriminators to compensation and possibly should be compensated even if the resources required would result in more welfare if used differently. Additionally, discriminators have a duty to respond to blame from those against whom they culpably discriminated, but possibly not to respond to blame from third parties (cf. Kolodny 2023, 18–19; May 2015; Srinivasan 2010).

Finally, discrimination might be wrongful for reasons by which only acts of discrimination are wrongful (Cavanagh 2002, 155). Alternatively, discrimination might be wrongful for non-distinctive reasons. If, for instance, discrimination is wrongful because of how it harms discriminatees, then because there are ways to harm people without discriminating against them, discriminatory acts would be wrongful for the same reasons as non-discriminatory acts. This does not imply that there is nothing special about the wrongfulness of discrimination. Discriminatory acts could be harmful in distinctive ways – for example, in the way they involve systematic and cumulative harms.

None of these three points directly answers the question of what makes discrimination wrongful. However, they clarify what sort of answers to the question we can expect. Sections 2–4 examine three direct answers to this question.

1.5 Methodological Preliminaries

Studies of wrongful discrimination are diverse in terms of their approach. Here I want to highlight three features of the approach adopted in this Element. There are good justifications for these features, but here I can do little more than simply articulate them, gesture at their attractions, and indicate how other theorists might differ.

First, I, along with some of the theorists that I discuss (e.g., see Section 2.5), often use hypothetical examples. Sometimes I use them to make a conceptual point – for example, to point out what follows from a particular definition or claim. In other cases, I use them to defend a moral claim – for example, I appeal to moral intuitions about a hypothetical example not involving a wrong which, say, should involve a moral wrong if a certain principle is correct, thus inferring that the principle is probably not correct. The use of hypothetical examples is extremely common in philosophy (Sorensen 1992). One advantage of their use is that a pair of real-life examples typically differ in a lot of potentially morally relevant ways, thus leaving us with no way of knowing, insofar as we evaluate them differently, what makes them morally different. Comparing a pair of hypothetical examples we can make sure that, by our stipulation, they only differ in terms of one potentially morally relevant dimension, and we thus stand a much better chance of being able to tell what makes them morally different (see the comparison of inegalitarian and egalitarian belief in Section 3.3).

That said, many are sceptical of hypothetical examples. Typically, such scepticism is rooted in scepticism about the use of hypothetical examples that deviate significantly from the real world (Elster 2011; Wilkes 1993). Our intuitions are calibrated to deal with the world as it is and we have little reason to trust intuitions pertaining to worlds very different from ours – for example, worlds in which persons can live their entire life in an experience machine. Or so the argument goes. Fortunately, most hypothetical examples in this Element do not involve imagining worlds very different from ours. Hence, if you share the stated scepticism about hypothetical examples, you should be on board with most of this Element's hypothetical examples anyway.

Second, some discrimination theorists think that there is an intimate connection between the philosophical analysis of discrimination, on one hand, and the lived experience of victims of discrimination, on the other hand (Beeghly 2023, 124–127; Moreau 2020). Often theorists who take this stance think that this speaks against using hypothetical examples.

There is some truth and some untruth to what is suggested here. There is a lot of truth to the view that to understand what makes a certain form of discrimination harmful (Onwuachi-Willig 2019) or wrong, and what might sensibly be done about it, one needs to listen attentively to (other) people subjected to the former and putatively benefitting, epistemically, from the latter (Moreau 2020, 28). Indeed, it might well be that they have a moral claim to be listened to even if, counterfactually, doing so would have no epistemic value. 'Nothing about us without us', as it is sometimes put.

However, there is also some untruth to the stance suggested here. First, to adopt the suggested approach, we need initially to determine which 'lived experiences' our theory should make sense of. Plausibly, some people – perhaps due to false consciousness – do not experience themselves as discriminatees, even if they are, and some people – for example, white males – see themselves as being unfairly discriminated against qua white males even if they are not. Hence, to adopt the present approach we need a prior identification of which experiences of discrimination are veridical and that requires a prior (revisable) view of wrongful discrimination. Second, it is unclear what it means for an account of wrongful discrimination to make sense of discriminatees' lived experience. If, say, a theory of discrimination is true to the lived experiences of discrimination if, and only if, it causally explains or correctly interprets these experiences, arguably this is a deliverable that a theory of wrongful discrimination is not in the business of providing. Perhaps a theory of the wrongful discrimination is true to the lived experiences of discriminatees if, and only if, what the theory identifies as making discrimination wrongful is identical to what, in the (possibly, hypothetically, better-informed) eyes of the discriminatees makes it wrongful. While I am open to being true to the lived experience of discrimination in this sense as a weak desideratum for a theory of wrongful discrimination, I do not think it undermines the project pursued in this Element. Victims of discrimination disagree about what makes the way in which they have been treated wrongful and this throws us back to philosophical arguments adjudicating these conflicting views. In so doing, the use of hypothetical examples might assist discriminatees in clarifying to themselves what, fundamentally, they find wrongful about their situation.

Finally, many discrimination theorists think that there is a close connection between discrimination law and philosophy of discrimination. For instance, they might think that law has some kind of privileged role in relation to determining what counts as discrimination such that if, say, a certain kind of differential treatment would not qualify as discrimination in the eyes of law, then that is a weakness of a definition of discrimination that implies that it is. There is a division of conceptual labour, as it were, and judges and legal theorists play a privileged role in that structure. Similarly, while legal theorists often engage, and very diligently so, in what essentially is a philosophical inquiry about the wrongfulness of discrimination, they often frame what they are doing as a matter of making sense of or reconstructing the ethical foundations or rationale for discrimination law (e.g., Hellman and Moreau 2013; Khaitan 2015, 4; Moreau 2020, 27–28). By their own lights then, their accounts of what makes discrimination morally wrongful are open to challenges based on the putative fact that an alternative and conflicting moral principle makes better sense of discrimination law. Also, some theorists grant a privileged epistemic status to law. Moreau (2020, 28), for instance, thinks that it is plausible that 'the basic features of antidiscrimination law will be sensitive to the morally objectionable features of these practices'.

While one can learn a lot about the nature and wrongfulness of discrimination from legal theorists (as is shown by the references) and from concrete court cases on discrimination, this Element makes no assumptions of the sort just indicated. This is justifiable, one important reason being that discrimination varies hugely across different countries and across time. Indeed, discrimination law is a relatively recent thing, and law itself (unlike legal philosophy) can provide reasons neither for why we should have such a thing as discrimination law, nor for which form such law should take. Moreover, the present point about the intimate connection between law and the philosophy of discrimination stands in some tension with the view that philosophy of discrimination should be true to the lived experience of marginalised minorities. One does not have to be Marxian to think that discrimination law is very much shaped by all sorts of factors other than the experience of marginalised minorities.

1.6 Conclusion

'To discriminate' has both a generic sense (differentiating) and several more specific ones. I identified the notion of group discrimination as the sense of discrimination that is the most fruitful one for the purposes of this Element (Section 1.2). Next, I distinguished between direct and indirect, statistical and non-statistical, and structural and non-structural discrimination (Section 1.3). I then clarified some issues in relation to what sort of answers we can expect to the question of what makes discrimination wrongful. Specifically, I distinguished between monism and pluralism, between discrimination being wrongful and morally impermissible, and between the wrongful-making feature of discrimination being distinct (Section 1.4). Finally, I highlighted some methodological assumptions of this Element, hopefully, pre-empting worries about its approach that some readers might otherwise have (Section 1.5). Section 2 examines what most would consider to be one important reason (and, according to some, the only reason) why wrongful discrimination is wrong: that discrimination harms discriminatees.

2 Harm

2.1 Introduction

Sections 2–4 survey three accounts of what makes discrimination wrongful, when it is. This section focuses on the harm-based account, according to which an instance of discrimination is wrongful, when it is, because the discriminator harms the discriminatee (or others). Sections 3 and 4 focus on the disrespect and the relational egalitarian accounts. Accounts other than these three exist – for example, that discrimination is wrongful because of how it violates norms of desert or merit (Miller 2001); detracts from freedom, understood as secured access to certain basic goods (Khaitan 2015, 244); involves failing to treat people as individuals (Beeghly 2023, 122–123; Lippert-Rasmussen 2011; Liu and Liang 2020; Thomas 1992); causes discriminatees to reasonably develop a sense of inferior political status (Hosein 2018); or increases inequality of opportunity (Segall 2012).

In normative ethics in general, there is no consensus on what features, if any (recall Section 1.4), make actions wrongful. While, in principle, such a high-level disagreement could exist alongside consensus on what makes discrimination wrongful, in fact it does not.

In this section, I first say something about the currency of harm and about the so-called pro tanto duty not to harm people and the wrongfulness of discrimination (Section 2.2). Next, I discuss when discriminatory actions harm discriminatees (Section 2.3). Third, I address the distributive principle underpinning the moral assessment of acts of discrimination in view of the harms and benefits they involve (Section 2.4). Finally, I present two kinds of counterexamples to the harm-based account (Section 2.5).

2.2 Why Does Harm Make Discrimination Wrongful?

The first question to ask in relation to a harm-based account of the wrongfulness of discrimination is why does the fact that it harms people make discrimination wrongful? This might seem like an odd question. Possibly, the most intuitively compelling moral duty is the pro tanto moral duty not to make other people's lives worse (Kagan 1989). (The fact that the duty is a pro tanto duty means that it is not an all-things-considered duty and that counterweighing considerations mean that sometimes we can permissibly harm others even if we have a pro tanto duty not to do so.) Accordingly, on the assumption that harms produced by discrimination make people's lives go worse, it seems to follow that we have a moral duty not to harm others through discrimination. Moreover, in the case of many acts other than acts of discrimination, what makes them wrongful is that they harm others. Why, for instance, do we have a moral duty not to physically aggress against other people? Plausibly, because in doing so we (generally) harm them. But if that is so, it is hard to see why we should not say something similar about acts of discrimination. We have a pro tanto moral reason not to harm others, which in specific cases in the absence of countervailing reasons that are at least as strong turns into an all-things-considered moral duty not to do what in the concrete instance amount to harming others. Hence, harmful acts of discrimination are at least pro tanto wrongful.

Unfortunately, this line of argument is flawed. First, not all instances of discrimination are harmful. As we saw in Section 1.3, direct discrimination involves disadvantageous treatment. But disadvantageous treatment is not the same as harmful treatment. If a sexist employer wrongfully rejects a female applicant who then because of the rejection lands a better job, the employer treats her disadvantageously and yet, plausibly, does not harm her overall (Eidelson 2015, 30–38). Arguably, such an act of discrimination is wrongful even if, overall, it turned out to be beneficial to the discriminatee.

Second, the harms involved in discrimination might accrue to the discriminatees, to the discriminator, or to third parties – that is, bystanders. It is unclear that all these harms bear on the wrongfulness or even the moral impermissibility of discrimination. Suppose members of the dominant religion discriminate against members of a specific religious minority group. Suppose this indirectly harms members of another religious minority group – perhaps members of the former minority often engage in economic transactions with members of the latter, and their being poorer because of direct discrimination against them restricts the quantity of goods they can buy from members of the bystander religious minority. Such harms count against the act of discrimination being morally permissible. However, they are not harms in virtue of which the discrimination is wrongful. At least these harms are irrelevant to why the discrimination in question wrongs the discriminatees, and it is not clear that members of the bystander religious minority are wronged when members of another minority are subjected to religious discrimination (Cornell 2015). Similarly, discriminators do not wrong themselves when they discriminate against others in ways that harm themselves.

Finally, typically when people think of harmful discriminatory acts, the sort of harm they have in mind – not being promoted, not getting a pay raise, not being admitted by a prestigious university – is not the sort of harm which the pro tanto duty not to harm others pertains to – that is, the harm of their lives not going as well as possible. Harms of the former type might well be generally associated with harms of the latter. However, the association is rough. Promotion might mean that one spends a greater proportion of one's life on work rather than on close social relations which are ultimately more important to one's well-being. Hence, if harm in the latter sense is the sense of harm which is crucial to wrongful action, then we should expect that once we identify cases where the two diverge, sometimes we must retract the assertion of wrongful discrimination – for example, when we learn that the candidate not promoted on discriminatory grounds does not lead a life that is worse as a result.

In sum, the thought that discrimination is wrongful because of the harms it involves is an appealing one. However, it becomes less forceful once we keep in mind instances of wrongful discrimination that appear not to be harmful in the relevant sense (more on this in Section 2.5), harms from discrimination accruing to actors other than the discriminatees, and the gap between the sense of harm invoked in complaints about wrongful discrimination versus the sense of harm involved in the relevant pro tanto duty not to harm others.

2.3 When Is Discrimination Harmful?

When does an act of discrimination harm a discriminatee? Like the opening question in Section 2.2, this seems like a silly question considering how acts of discrimination are often obviously harmful. However, once we scratch the surface, we see that the notion of harming is tricky and that how we resolve the puzzles it involves has important implications for what the harm-based account implies. Consider:

> *Overdetermination*: Suzy applies for a job. The hiring committee has five members, any of whom can veto any candidate. Two members of the committee, Andrew and Burt, are misogynists and thus both veto Suzy on grounds of her gender. Had neither Andrew nor Burt vetoed Suzy's being hired, Suzy would have gotten the job.

In this case, Andrew and Burt engage in wrongful sex discrimination against Suzy. Yet there is a case for saying that neither of them harm Suzy. The outcome would have been the same – Suzy would not have gotten the job – if Andrew or alternatively Burt had not engaged in sexist discrimination against Suzy. At least this follows if we accept the *counterfactual notion of harming* according to which a agent harms a victim by their act if, and only if, the victim would have been better off had the agent not performed this act.

This view might seem appealing, and it is the one which often underpins our identification of harmful acts. However, *someone* harms Suzy in overdetermination, and yet it is not clear that this view is compatible with the counterfactual notion of harm.

There are different ways to respond to this problem. First, one might stick to the counterfactual notion of harm and submit that the group consisting of

Andrew and Burt did harm Suzy. If they had both acted differently, no harm would have occurred (Parfit 1986, 70). While this move accommodates overdetermination, it is unclear that one could not tweak it such that the counterfactual notion of harm applied to group agents will imply, implausibly, that no agent harms the victim. For instance, we could tweak the case by stipulating that some computer mishap would have occurred if neither Andrew nor Burt had vetoed Suzy, resulting in Suzy still not being hired.

Second, one can go for the *non-counterfactual notion of harm* according to which an agent harms a victim by their act if, and only if, there is a relevant causal chain leading from the agent's action to some bad for the victim (cf. Berndt Rasmussen 2019, 886). Much here hangs on what one means by 'relevant causal chain'. It could be fleshed out in different ways. On one such way, if five persons simultaneously push a car and two would have sufficed to make the car move, then each of them pushing the car is a partial cause of the car moving. Their contribution to the outcome is proportional to the share of the force they exert on the car which causes it to move (Tadros 2018, 408). One motivation for this is that even if the push of two persons would have sufficed for making the car move, it would be arbitrary to point to any two of these individuals and say that their pushes, unlike those of the three others, caused the car to move. Perhaps this notion of harm can be developed in such a way that the harm-based account can accommodate overdetermination.

There is a second problem regarding when discriminatory acts are harmful. This problem pertains to the extent to which we should treat the discriminatory actions of others as given when we assess whether a given discriminatory action harmed the discriminatee (Lippert-Rasmussen 2013, 157–160). Consider:

> *Mixed Motivation Sexist Employer.* Claude has advertised a position for a marketing director at his company. Suzy is the best qualified applicant. However, Claude refuses to hire her, partly because he recoils at the idea of a female boss, and partly because he knows that since all the other bosses in his company are sexists, it would be bad for Suzy to get the job.

Suppose Claude is accused of harmful, sexist discrimination. Can he dismiss this complaint on the ground that it would have been bad for Suzy to have gotten the job? After all, because Claude's company is permeated with sexism, Suzy would have been worse off getting the job than she would have been without getting it. In making this claim, we hold constant the wrongful discriminatory actions of others. In effect, this implies that the more disposed others are to engage in harmful discriminatory actions, the harder it is for people like Claude to commit a wrongfully harmful sexist act of discrimination. Possibly, if enough people are disposed to act in discriminatory ways, then even if the overall pattern of actions is clearly discriminatory, there are no single harmful discriminatory acts – for example, because of the harms imposed on people who do not conform to gender roles, sexist decisions which enforce those roles are always for the better of these people.

There are two ways to respond to this problem. First, like in the response to the problem of overdetermination, one could shift the focus from how individual acts of discriminatory action harm individuals to how patterns of actions – that is, social structures – harm individuals (see Section 1.3). Second, one could adopt a moralised baseline for the purpose of determining whether a given discriminatory act is harmful. Hence, for the purpose of determining whether Suzy was harmed by Claude's refusal to hire her, we should compare what happened to a situation in which she was hired, and her sexist colleagues had not engaged in wrongful acts of discrimination against her. Relative to *that* baseline, she was harmed for not being hired. The problem is that for the purpose of guiding Claude's action, it is unclear what relevance this baseline has. If, while stranded on a desert island, I could have opened some tin food cans washed ashore if (and only if) I had had a tin opener, that gives me no reason to pick up the tin cans given that I do not have a tin opener. In sum: it is a surprisingly complex matter when discrimination is harmful.

2.4 The Distribution of Harm

Harm-based accounts of the wrongfulness of discrimination face another challenge. Virtually all actions both harm and benefit some people. Suppose that if an action imposes a harm on you which is sufficiently small relative to the much greater benefits that the same act confers on a great number of people, then that action does not wrong you. Had you been able to consent to being subjected to the relevant harm, you would have been under a moral duty to do so. That supposition seems plausible. Consider:

> *Cabin*: Beatrice is about to die in a snowstorm in the mountains. The only way she can survive is by breaking into your cabin, which she does.

Even if her doing so harms you slightly – say, she cannot compensate you for the window she breaks by entering the cabin – in light of the great benefit to her and small harm to you, she not only acts morally permissibly by breaking into your cabin; she does not treat you wrongfully. If, as I have just suggested, this supposition is plausible, and if any act causes both harms and benefits to countless people, then a harm-based account of wrongful discrimination must involve a principle telling us how to weigh the harms and benefits involved in a discriminatory act to determine whether it is wrongful.

There are several candidates here. One suggestion is that if the benefits exceed the harms, then the relevant harm does not make the discrimination in question wrongful. However, arguably this view is too simple because it does not consider how well off the discriminatee and the beneficiaries of discrimination are. Compare:

> *Worse-Off Discriminatee*: Suzy is badly off. Discriminating against her harms her slightly, while it benefits some very well-off beneficiaries greatly.
> *Better-Off Discriminatee*: Suzy is very well off. Discriminating against her imposes a small disadvantage on her, while it benefits some very badly off beneficiaries greatly.

Possibly Suzy is wrongfully discriminated against in the first case but not in the second, even if the harms and benefits involved are equal in size. If so, this means that distribution matters to whether harmful discrimination is wrongful and, thus, that a harm-based account of wrongful discrimination is tied to a background theory of distributive justice.

There are two ways in which distribution matters to whether harmful discrimination is wrongful. First, it might matter as such. We might think equality is intrinsically valuable, and the reason that we should assess the worse-off and better-off discriminatees differently is that in the former discrimination increases inequality, while in the latter it reduces it. Alternatively, we might say that distribution does not matter as such. However, it matters indirectly to the strength of the moral claims to avoiding the harms and receiving the benefits in question how well off the recipients are. On a prioritarian view, the reason we should assess the worse-off and better-off discriminatees differently is in part that Suzy's claim to avoid the harm in question varies depending on whether she is badly or very well off and in part because the strength of the moral claims of the potential beneficiaries similarly varies with how well off they are (Arneson 1999; Lippert-Rasmussen 2013).

2.5 Wrongless Harmful Discrimination and Harmless Wrongful Discrimination

The harm-based account says that discrimination is wrongful because of the harm it involves. Hence, it can face two kinds of counterexamples: instances of discrimination which are harmful but not wrongful, and instances that are wrongful but harmless. These counterexamples have different upshots. The first suggests that it is not harm, but other features, that makes discrimination wrongful. The second counterexample suggests that harm is not the only wrong-making feature of discrimination, even if it might be one among several. Let us start with the first counterexample:

> *Consensual Age Discrimination*: Healthcare is organised such that, at the age of eighteen, one chooses between being assigned to either of two groups of patients: one where doctors will give priority to younger patients and another where doctors will disregard age. The number of resources available per person in the two groups is the same. Patients in the former group have a higher number of expected quality-adjusted life-years than patients in the latter. However, members of the first group risk being denied treatment on grounds of their old age.

Arguably, consensual age discrimination involves a case of harmful, non-wrongful discrimination. Given that the victims of harmful age discrimination have validly consented to being subjected to it, whether or not consensual discrimination is in some sense morally bad, it does not wrong consenting discriminatees (but see Bengtson and Munch 2024). In consenting to being exposed to the risk of age discrimination in the interest of maximising their expected quality-adjusted life-years, they validly waived their rights against harmful age discrimination in the relevant context.

One might take consensual age discrimination to suggest that while there is no right against harm per se, there is a right against *non-consensual* harm. However, intuitively, there is no such general right either. If, without my consent as it were, you apply for a job that I have already applied for, so that I am no longer the best-qualified applicant and you get the job, you have harmed me. However, I have no right against you not harming me in this way. Hence, at most one has a right not to be non-consensually harmed *in certain ways*, and these ways are determined by considerations other than considerations about harm – for example, a theory of justice. If so, then the harm-based account rests on a prior account of what kinds of harm one has a right not to be subjected to.

Moving on to the second kind of counterexample – cases of wrongful but harmless discrimination – consider:

> *Cambridge University*: Helen is an admissions officer at Cambridge University. As a result of her racist prejudices, she is averse to spending time around students with dark skin tone ... [S]he believes that it would be wrong for her to harm these applicants, so she uses her connections to ensure that all those applicants that she rejects on racist grounds secure a place at Oxford. (The places Helen secures for these students are *additional* ones such that no one else is denied a place at Oxford as a result of Helen's actions.) Applicants are indifferent between Oxford and Cambridge, and they would not have received an offer from Oxford but for Helen's intervention. (Slavny and Parr 2015, 105–106)

According to Slavny and Parr, this is a case of harmless wrongful discrimination (cf. Section 2.3). Thus, if Helen's act is wrong, as Slavny and Parr believe it is, then some moral factor other than harm must explain this. Slavny and Parr believe that factor is disrespect (Section 3).

Cases like this put pressure on those who claim that the wrongfulness of discrimination is all about harm, but not on those who think it is *also* a matter of the harm involved in discrimination. However, it is not as if friends of an exclusively harm-based account have no responses to cases like this. First, our moral intuitions about the case might reflect intuitions about Helen's moral character, and not the wrongfulness of Helen's discriminatory action. Consider a variant of this Cambridge University case, where the applicants in question have applied to Oxford University – Helen mistakenly believes that they have applied to Cambridge University. In this case, Helen has made it the case that applicants received what they applied for and, let us suppose, what they would have received in the absence of Helen's intervention. Helen has a bad character in this case as well. However, it is less clear that the applicants can complain that she has treated them wrongfully. If they have a right that Helen not think of them in a racist way, they have been wronged. However, rights over how others think of us independently of how they treat us are contentious (Sher 2022; see also Lippert-Rasmussen and Vallentyne forthcoming). Additionally, if we have such rights, then perhaps we can be harmed by others simply thinking of us in a racist way. If so, perhaps the right not to be thought of in a racist way is grounded in the dignitarian harm that our being thought of in this way imposed on us (Arneson 2017, 157; Thomsen 2023, 440; cf. Laborde 2024; Slavny and Parr 2015, 109). Second, it is unclear that disrespect explains the wrongfulness involved in this Cambridge University scenario. An alternative explanation, which incidentally would not rescue the harm-based account unless supplemented, appeals to Helen's violation of her professional duties (Thomsen 2023, 440; cf. Slavny and Parr 2015, 111).

2.6 Conclusion

Section 2 has focused on explanations of the wrongfulness of discrimination, appealing to how discrimination is harmful. Despite the account's intuitive appeal, once we begin to fill in the details, the harm-based account becomes surprisingly complex and problematic. Specifically, I described two kinds of counterexamples to the account. One suggests that, ultimately, a defensible harm-based account rests on a prior account of what harms discriminatees have a right not to be subjected to, while the other suggests that harm is not the only wrong-making feature. Hence, the harm-based account of the wrongfulness of discrimination is neither an obviously correct nor an obviously incorrect account. As we shall see in Section 3, the same can be said about the so-called respect-based account.

3 Disrespect

3.1 Introduction

The most influential alternative to the harm-based account is:

> *The Disrespect-Based Account*: An instance of discrimination is wrongful, when it is, because the discriminator disrespects the discriminatee (or others).

What it is to disrespect someone is tricky. Supposedly to disrespect someone is not the same as harming them. If it were, then the harm- and disrespect-based accounts would be no different. This is neither to say that there could not be ways of harming someone which are disrespectful in virtue of being harmful, nor to say there could not be ways of being disrespectful that harm those subjected to disrespect. However, it is to say that either there are ways to harm people which do not disrespect them, or there are ways of disrespecting people which do not harm them – for example, successful paternalistic discrimination (Midtgaard and Pedersen 2024).

Just as disrespecting is different from harming, disrespecting someone is different from forming an unfavourable attitude towards them – for example, disliking someone on account of their being arrogant. Stephen Darwall (1977, 38) distinguishes between appraisal and recognition respect. The former pertains to 'persons or features which are held to manifest their excellence as persons or as engaged in some specific pursuit'. The latter 'consists in giving appropriate consideration or recognition to some feature of its object in deliberating about what to do'. While discrimination might involve both forms of disrespect, friends of the disrespect-based account appeal to the latter, if to either. Specifically, they appeal to the idea that wrongful discrimination fails to give appropriate consideration to the discriminatee's personhood. Disliking someone on account of their being arrogant might involve appraisal disrespect, but it does not involve a failing to appropriately consider the arrogant individual's personhood.

I first examine why a discriminator's failure to give appropriate consideration and recognition to someone's personhood is wrongful (Section 3.2). Next, I discuss three different theories of disrespectful discrimination: Larry Alexander's and Ben Eidelson's mental state-based accounts (Sections 3.3 and 3.4) and Deborah Hellman's social meaning-based account (Section 3.5). All three appeal to the idea of equality of moral status of persons. Hence, Section 3.6 examines that elusive notion and how it might (not) explain the disrespectfulness and, thus, wrongfulness of discrimination. Finally, Section 3.7 considers two counterexamples to the disrespect-based account: cases of wrongless disrespectful discrimination and of disrespectless wrongful discrimination.

3.2 Why Does Disrespect Make an Act Wrongful?

Just as we can ask why a person is wronged by being harmed, we can ask why a person is wronged by someone who fails to give 'appropriate consideration and recognition' to the fact that they are persons. It is not true of any fact about a person that if others fail to give 'consideration and recognition' to it, they wrong them. I am a philosopher who has written extensively on discrimination, who thoroughly likes Corsica, and who grew up in the Danish town of Odense. Virtually no one gives any consideration to or recognition of these facts. But they do not wrong me for that reason.

Some might reply that this is because, generally, the *appropriate* consideration and recognition of *these* facts about me, like most other facts about me except, for example, for the fact that I am a person, is none. While this response is appealing, it gives rise to a new question: what makes the fact that I am a person a fact about me that, generally, is relevant to most interactions with others, unlike the fact that I am a philosopher, like Corsica, etcetera? An appealing answer is that my being a person, unlike my being a philosopher, liking Corsica, etcetera, generally matters for how I should be treated. Hence, if someone fails to give 'appropriate consideration and recognition' to the fact that I am a person, they are likely to treat me in ways that I ought not to be treated.

But if that is the reason we wrong people by failing to give appropriate consideration and recognition to the fact they are persons, what should we then say about an agent who fails to do so, but who nevertheless treats people in the way they ought to be treated, morally speaking? Consider an agent who values treating people whom they think of as non-persons in the way morality requires persons to be treated. Given the present explanation, they appear not to wrong those whom they disrespect.

There are two ways to respond to this. First, it might be said that treating persons as they should be treated without giving appropriate consideration and recognition to the fact that they are persons is impossible, because what morality requires is that persons are treated in certain ways, where the treatment in question is motivated in a way which involves giving appropriate consideration and recognition to the fact that they are persons. Second, friends of the respect-based account might say that independently of how others treat us, we have rights over how we figure in their deliberations such that, independently of the treatment these deliberations result in, agents have a duty to give appropriate consideration and recognition to the fact that the rightsholder is a person in their deliberations. As noted previously, the latter reply is controversial. Many deny that we owe anything to others regarding the unexpressed contents of our minds. The former reply is less controversial, and its proponents can point to the doctrine of the double effect as another moral principle inter alia which many accept and which implies that the wrongfulness of an action can depend on how it is motivated – for example, whether the harm involved is intended or merely foreseen.

3.3 False Beliefs about Moral Status

I now turn to the question of what it is to disrespect someone. In his early work on discrimination, Alexander (1992, 159) submits that when 'a person is judged incorrectly to be of lesser moral worth and is treated accordingly, that treatment . . . represents a failure to show the moral respect due to the recipient, a failure which is by itself sufficient to be judged immoral'. This view is appealing in light of cases such as a Nazi discriminating against someone they take to be an *Untermensch*. The drawback of it is that most putatively disrespectful instances of discrimination appear not to involve any such belief. Many unreflective, disrespectful discriminators have no beliefs about the comparative moral status of people.

Another problem is that it is unclear that disrespect is closely tied to *false* beliefs about moral status. Suppose – counterfactually if you like – that animals and human beings have the same moral status. Given that supposition, compare two experimenters who conduct painful experiments on animals that confer minor benefits on human beings:

> *Inegalitarian Belief*: The experimenter conducts his experiments on animals under the false but non-culpably formed belief that human beings have greater moral worth than animals. He picks his experimental objects partly on the basis of a desire to conform to social expectations, but reckons he would have chosen differently had he believed that animals and human beings have equal moral status.
>
> *Egalitarian Belief*: The experimenter conducts his experiments on animals while correctly and non-culpably believing that animals and human beings have equal moral worth. He picks his experimental objects partly on the basis of a desire to conform to social expectations, but reckons that he would have chosen differently had he believed that animals have higher moral status than human beings.

If Alexander's account is correct, the inegalitarian experimenter acts in a way that is disrespectful – he harms animals based on a (by stipulation) false, non-culpably formed belief about the unequal moral status of animals and human beings – unlike the egalitarian experimenter, who holds true beliefs about the comparative moral status of animals and human beings and yet singles out animals for the experiments. Since the two cases are identical in terms of harmful consequences, and since only Inegalitarian Belief involves Alexanderian disrespect, this case should be more wrongful than the other. However, *if* there is a difference in terms of wrongfulness between the two cases, Egalitarian Belief appears morally more wrong. However, on Alexander's account Inegalitarian Belief is wrongful in a way in which Egalitarian Belief is not – that is, it involves treating some worse than others on the basis of false beliefs about their moral status. And since the two cases are morally identical in terms of all other wrongful-making properties, on Alexander's account Inegalitarian Belief should be more wrongful – that is, the reasons that make it wrongful are stronger.

In response, friends of the view that it is possible to wrong people simply by holding certain beliefs about them (Basu 2019a, 2019b, 2019c, 2023a, 2023b; Basu and Schroeder 2018; Fabre 2022; Schroeder 2018) might suggest that because the inegalitarian, unlike the egalitarian, experimenter wrongs animals simply by holding false beliefs about their comparative moral status, there is one dimension on which the former is worse and thus it is unclear which of the two experimenters' actions is morally more wrong if one is more wrong than the other. However, the view that one can wrong someone simply by holding a false belief about them is not Alexander's. Merely doing that does not amount to *treating* one's object of belief in any way, so even if the present challenge points to something important it cannot be employed in defence of *Alexander's* position. Also, as already noted, it is controversial whether holding a certain false belief about a person wrongs that person. Specifically, the view that non-human animals can be wronged simply by people holding false belief of certain kind about them (as opposed to treating them badly motivated by these false beliefs) is a much stronger and less plausible view. Hence I conclude that if Alexander's account captures the essence of disrespect and if my claim about the conditional comparative wrongfulness of Egalitarian Belief and Inegalitarian Belief is correct, this generates problems for disrespect-based accounts in general. Perhaps this just shows that we should adopt an understanding of disrespect different from Alexander's.

3.4 Disrespect and Deliberative Failure

Like Alexander, Ben Eidelson (2015, 73) thinks that some acts 'of discrimination are intrinsically wrong when and because they manifest a failure to show the discriminatees the respect that is due to them as persons'. However, he conceives of disrespect differently from Alexander in that he appeals to Stephen Darwall's view that recognition respect amounts to 'a disposition to weigh appropriately in one's deliberations some feature of the thing in question and act accordingly' (Eidelson 2015, 76). According to Eidelson, two such features are crucial: (1) that 'persons are of value in themselves, and equally so', and (2) that 'persons are autonomous: they possess a faculty of self-control through which they can make their lives, in significant part, their own' (Eidelson 2015, 79).

By tying disrespect to a certain kind of deliberative failure instead of explicit beliefs about moral status, Eidelson's account has a broader scope than Alexander's and extends beyond ideologically motivated deniers of moral equality like Alexander's Nazi discriminator. An act can be disrespectful on Eidelson's account while not being disrespectful on Alexander's. Suppose that, despite my belief that men and women have equal moral worth, I suffer from an implicit bias such that I give greater weight to the interests of men than those of women. On Eidelson's account, unlike Alexander's, in so doing I act disrespectfully. This speaks in favour of Eidelson's account.

Nevertheless, Eidelson's account of disrespect is vulnerable to the pair of examples offered against Alexander's account earlier in this section. The egalitarian experimenter does not to a greater degree than the inegalitarian experimenter fail to give proper weight to the interests of animals, in part because both experimenters give less weight to the interests of animals in their deliberations than they should, assuming that animals and persons have the same moral status, in part because the egalitarian experimenter correctly acknowledges the comparative moral status of animals. Yet Eidelson thinks that what the egalitarian experimenter does is more wrongful. Accordingly, to accommodate the pair of counterexamples he introduces a notion of contempt:

> [C]ontempt seems to involve a refusal to respect something – a kind of defiance of what you at some level realize its significance to be ... it is too charitable to think of most textbook racists as simply holding false beliefs about the value or moral status of those whom they disfavor ... the genocidaires in Rwanda clearly did not mistake Tutsis for the evaluative equivalents of cockroaches ... Rather, they chose to treat them *as if* they were. (Eidelson 2015, 105)

Given three assumptions, the introduction of contempt is helpful. First, greater disrespect results in being morally more wrong, ceteris paribus. Second, contemptuous disrespect is more disrespectful than non-contemptuous disrespect, ceteris paribus. Third, egalitarian belief involves contemptuous disrespect – the experimenter at some level realises that human beings and animals have equal moral status and yet he treats animals as if they have a lower moral status – whereas inegalitarian belief only involves non-contemptuous disrespect. Given these assumptions, it follows that the egalitarian experimenter's act is more disrespectful and for that reason is more wrongful, even if both agents act disrespectfully by failing to give the interests of animals proper weight in their deliberations. Hence, provided that the three assumptions are correct, Eidelson's amended account is immune to the counterexample which defeats Alexander's account. Are they correct?

The first assumption is plausible. Disrespect comes in different degrees, and, given that disrespect is a wrong-making feature of actions, greater disrespect plausibly results in greater wrongness. The second assumption – that is, that contemptuous disrespect is more disrespectful than non-contemptuous disrespect – is not obviously true. While contempt in an ordinary sense is more disrespectful than non-contemptuous disrespect, it is unclear that Eidelsonian contempt is more disrespectful. After all, it involves *some* recognition of the moral status of the individual whom you hold in contempt (Eidelson 2015, 106). The slaveholder who truly believes that his slaves are subhuman is, in one respect, worse than the slaveholder who believes that his slaves are his moral equals, but then goes on to 'willfully reject' their human equality.

Consider the third assumption. Suppose that contempt also involves ill will and epistemic flaws in deliberations. That might render the second assumption more defensible. However, it undermines the third assumption, since differential hostility and epistemic flaws are not part of the counterexample to Alexander. Moreover, non-contemptuous disrespect can also involve hostility. Accordingly, if we want to test whether contemptuous disrespect is worse than non-contemptuous disrespect, we should stipulate that neither, or both, the inegalitarian and the egalitarian experimenter are hostile towards their experimental objects. Similarly, if the experimenter in egalitarian belief is somehow epistemically blameworthy for choosing animals as if they had a lower moral status when, at some level, he knows this not to be the case, then we should stipulate that the experimenter in *inegalitarian belief* is similarly flawed – that is, the inegalitarian experimenter is somehow epistemically blameworthy for choosing animals as if they had a lower moral status when, at some level and despite his explicit and false belief to the effect that human beings have a higher moral status than animals, he knows this not to be the case. Hence, it is unclear whether all three assumptions needed to enable Eidelson's account to accommodate my pair of counterexamples are true.

3.5 Objective Demeaningness

According to both Alexander and Eidelson, disrespect is a matter of the mental state of the discriminator. I now shift attention to Hellman's objective-meaning account. On this account, a discriminatory act is wrong when and because it demeans, where whether it demeans depends on whether a reasonable interpretation of its meaning is that it is demeaning (Beeghly 2017, 87; Hellman 2008). The meaning expressed by a discriminatory act depends on the objectively best interpretation of the relevant act in its specific cultural context at a specific time and is not fixed by the meaning the agent ascribes to it (Hellman 2008, 36).

In Hellman's account, not all discrimination that is expressive of disrespect is demeaning. Wrongful discrimination is differential treatment that *demeans* the discriminatee. A treatment demeans someone if, and only if, the following conditions are satisfied. First, the relevant individual is treated as 'not of equal moral worth' (Hellman 2008, 8). Second, the discriminator must be hierarchically superior to or enjoy power over the discriminatee. A boss can demean an employee, but, in the absence of some employment-unrelated power or status difference, an employee cannot demean her boss. An employee might succeed in making a boss feel humiliated, but that is a perlocutionary effect of an act of demeaning. That act itself is an illocutionary act, which can only be performed by an agent who stands in a specific social relation to the person subjected to the act – for example, only a guardian can consent on a child's behalf.

Discrimination that demeans is wrong because it clashes with the 'bedrock moral principle' of the equal moral worth of persons (Hellman 2008, 6): 'the point of equality is to treat one another as equals, and thus the wrong of discrimination is to fail to treat people as equals. We do that when we differentiate among people in a manner that ranks some as less morally worthy than others' (Hellman 2008, 172). The principle of equal moral worth consists of two sub-principles. The first says that 'there is a worth or inherent dignity in persons that requires that we treat each other with respect' (Hellman 2008, 6). The second says that 'this inherent dignity and worth of all persons does not vary according to their other traits'. By implication, 'all people are equally important from the moral point of view and so are equally worthy of concern and respect' (Hellman 2008, 6).

Is Hellman's account an improvement over Alexander's and Eidelson's? First, because Hellman ties her account to a denial of the 'bedrock' principle of moral equality, this might render it plausible (see also Section 3.6). However, the cost is that many acts which, intuitively, are disrespectful are not clearly disrespectful in Hellman's sense. Consider the following case discussed by Hellman:

> *Nelson Mandela's Autobiography*: the apartheid regime in South Africa required black prisoners to wear shorts while white and colored prisoners were required to wear pants [long trousers]. In the heat of southern Africa, shorts might be the more comfortable option. Nonetheless, the symbolism of being required to wear

shorts, which were commonly seen as infantilizing in this postcolonial regime, was a means of demeaning black prisoners. (Hellman 2008, 5)

These differential requirements were disrespectful because of the infantilisation involved. But, first, when assessing cases of demeaning discrimination, it is natural to assume that they negatively affect those who are demeaned. However, on Hellman's account this is not what makes such cases morally wrongful. What does so is the mere fact that the cases have a specific demeaning cultural meaning. To assess the plausibility of this view, we should therefore consider an act of demeaning discrimination that *benefits* discriminatees by an agent who intends to confer those benefits on the discriminatees and has no other option than to do so through an act whose objective cultural meaning is demeaning. Arguably, this agent might not even be doing something which is disrespectful or pro tanto wrongful.

Second, suppose that those who perform actions that are objectively demeaning are non-culpably unaware of the cultural meaning of their act. Do they disrespect those whom they demean? Even if there is a sense in which those who are subjected to demeaning treatment live in a social world where they are disrespected, it seems no individual agent disrespects them. Consider an analogy: I am being asked to convey an unopened letter to a recipient with a disrespectful message. I am not aware, and cannot be faulted for not so being, of the disrespectful content of the letter. Plausibly, I am not disrespecting the addressee by delivering the letter, even though it might be true that the addressee is being disrespected. If so, this gives rise to the question of whether such agentless disrespect is wrongful or, if it is not, how it is possible for something to be wrongful in the absence of a perpetrator.

3.6 Moral Equality and Disrespect

As noted, all three disrespect-based accounts considered tie disrespect to a denial of the equal moral worth of persons. To test this connection, consider:

The Polis of Coincidental Equality: In an ancient Greek polis, everyone thought that being male and being able-bodied boosted one's moral status – and did so to an equal degree. All men were disabled and all women not. Hence everyone related to everyone else as if they were of equal moral status. However, any individual has a property that other polis members treat as if it reduces the moral status of the bearer relative to non-bearers. But because the status-affecting properties counterbalance one another, having a particular status-reducing property never results in the bearer having a lower moral status than any other.

No doubt this polis involves a strange coincidence. But it is possible. And this suffices for the two points the case supports. First, the polis involves disrespectful treatment of everyone – for example, I disrespect you if I treat you as if you have a lower moral status in virtue of your gender or (dis)ability status. To explain this, we cannot appeal to the moral equality of persons, since ex hypothesis everyone is treated as if they possess that. Instead, we might appeal to:

> *The Irrelevant Property Account*: Discrimination is disrespectful and thus wrongful when it involves treating discriminatees as if a property of theirs reduces the moral status of the property bearer relative to non-bearers when that property makes no such difference. (Lippert-Rasmussen 2023a)

The irrelevant property account does not imply that all persons have equal moral status. Moreover, unlike the appeal to moral equality of all persons, it explains why people are disrespected in the polis of coincidental equality.

Second, the polis of coincidental equality shows that the concept of disrespect is not 'inherently comparative' across different individuals in the way our three theorists assume. On Hellman's (2008, 172) view, what 'fuels' our opposition to discrimination is that it demeans by differentiating 'among people in a manner that ranks some as less morally worthy than others'. Differentiation of this sort does not occur in my Greek polis. Yet it does involve disrespectful discrimination. Thus, we can have disrespect without denial of or disregard for the moral equality of persons!

3.7 Wrongless Disrespectful Discrimination and Disrespectless Wrongful Discrimination

The disrespect-based account says that discrimination is wrongful because disrespectful. Hence it can face two kinds of counterexamples: instances of discrimination which are disrespectful but not wrongful, and instances which are wrongful but disrespectless. Counterexamples of both kinds are powerful, albeit not decisive.

First, arguably there are instances of discrimination that are wrongful but not disrespectful. Consider cases of indirect or structural discrimination (Section 1.3) which disadvantage members of certain minorities, where the policies in question are not informed by disrespectful mental states, nor bear any demeaning cultural meaning – for example, because the causal connections involved have no cultural meaning that a well-placed interpreter can uncover. Like with the analogous counterexample to the harm-based account, this counterexample does not show that disrespect does not render discrimination wrongful – only that it is not the only factor that does so.

Second, there are instances of discrimination that are disrespectful, but not wrongful. I have already considered the case of an agent who performs an act whose cultural meaning is demeaning, but where the agent does so only to benefit those whom the act demeans. This action is disrespectful on Hellman's account. Yet it appears not to be wrongful. I also considered a pair of examples that together form an anomaly on Alexander's account – that is, Egalitarian and Inegalitarian Belief, where the case which, on Alexander's account, is disrespectful was less wrongful than the other. Finally, I suggested that Eidelson's invocation of contempt does not save his account from a related set of counterexamples.

3.8 Conclusion

Section 3 has focused on the disrespect account. Despite its appeal, it is unclear what exactly disrespect involves. Like with the harm-based account, I have described two kinds of counterexamples to the account. One supports that disrespect is not the only wrong-making feature of discrimination. Perhaps many sympathetic to the disrespect-based account would welcome a pluralist account of the wrongfulness of discrimination. The other counterexample suggests that, ultimately, we still have not identified a plausible account of what disrespect amounts to such that we can plausibly say that any act of disrespectful discrimination is for that reason wrongful. Hence, like the harm-based account, the disrespect-based account is neither obviously correct nor clearly incorrect. In Section 4, we will consider one final contender: the relational egalitarian account.

4 Social Equality

4.1 Introduction

For many years, political philosophers assumed that justice is a matter of the proper distribution of some good. On their view, the hard questions are what that good is (e.g., resources or well-being) and what the principle regulating the distribution of that good is (e.g., equality, priority, or sufficiency). However, relational egalitarian theorists like Iris Marion Young, Elizabeth Anderson, and Samuel Scheffler have argued that the distributive approach to justice is flawed. On their view, fundamentally justice is a matter of whether people relate socially to each other as equals, and many injustices cannot be analysed in terms of a skewed distribution. Indeed, wrongful, racist discrimination against a distributively speaking privileged racial minority could realise the putative aims of distributive justice – for example, an equal distribution of resources. Cases like this show, according to relational egalitarians, that even if distributive egalitarians might in some sense subscribe to the ideal of treating people equal at a very abstract level – in their view, all have equal initial claims to the goods that distributive justice concerns – they ascribe no fundamental significance to social relations being egalitarian. Hence, we might favour:

> *The Relational Egalitarian Account* (for short: *The Relational Account*): An instance of discrimination is wrongful, when it is, because the discriminator fails to relate to the discriminatee (or others) as an equal.

The most immediate question this account faces is what relating as equals amounts to. Certain ways of harming or disrespecting others – for example, enslaving them – plausibly amount to not relating to them as equals. However, arguably one can also harm and even disrespect others without relating to them as unequals – recall the polis of coincidental equality (Section 3.6). Also, there are ways of not relating as equals that do not involve harming or disrespecting others – for example, relating to others as if one was inferior to those with whom one relates.

Painting with a broad brush, one can distinguish between two different answers to the question of what it means to relate as (un)equals. One says that the concept is well defined and thus that to explore the commitments of relational egalitarianism we should engage in analysing the notion of relating as equals (Lippert-Rasmussen 2018, 61–93). Another view says that 'relating as (un)equals' is largely a placeholder for the social relations that relational egalitarians (dis)favour. On this view, domination might be incompatible with relating as equals, but this is not something we can infer from an analysis of the concept of relating as equals. Rather, it is something we can infer from the fact that such relations are condemned by those who identify as relational egalitarians.

In this section, I look at an approach of the latter kind. More specifically, I examine Sophia Moreau's relational egalitarian account of the wrongfulness of discrimination. First, I address the question of why it is wrongful not to relate as equals (Section 4.2). Next, I examine three ways in which we can fail to do so (Section 4.3). Section 4.4 explores how the distinction between moral and social equality bears on the wrongfulness of discrimination. Section 4.5 looks at two possible counterexamples to the relational egalitarian account.

4.2 Why Is It Wrongful Not to Relate as Equals?

On Moreau's view, what troubles us about discrimination is that 'some people are treated as *inferiors*' (Moreau 2020, 8, 218–232). Why is one wronged if one is treated as inferior? In response to this question, many are likely to appeal to certain empirical facts about all human beings in virtue of which they have equal moral status – for example, the capacity to reason and see oneself and others as moral agents. However, it is difficult to point to universally shared capacities plausibly conferring the same moral status on all. Some human beings cannot reason, nor see themselves as moral agents. Moreover, where these capacities exist they come in degrees, suggesting that some of us have higher moral status than others and thus suggesting perhaps that we should not relate as equals. In response to concerns such as these, Moreau submits that 'it is a mistake to search for a deeper foundation for our belief in each person's equal moral status. Any argument that tries to locate such a foundation will have to appeal to claims that we are less certain about, and more readily willing to abandon, than our conviction that we are all each other's equals' (Moreau 2020, 223). One might worry, however, that even if, initially, we are less willing to abandon our commitment to moral equality than anything else, there must be some non-moral facts about those who enjoy equal moral worth from which this moral property of theirs results in a metaphysical sense. If there are no good candidates for what those facts are, an insistence that we are all of equal moral worth becomes dogmatic.

Nevertheless, Moreau suggests an argument for why the state should treat all of its citizens as equals by positing equal moral status: 'We are all of equal moral value. Consequently, the state has a duty to treat each person whom it governs as the equal of every other person whom it governs' (Moreau 2020, 225). Perhaps there is something to an argument like this. However, *does* the premise entail the conclusion? One question here is whether the phrase 'treating as the equal' in the conclusion refers to something the state does if, and only if, it treats each person that it governs as if they are of equal moral value. Relational egalitarians might face a dilemma here. If, on one hand, one specifies that the equality in the conclusion is simply that, the inference looks less obviously unsound, but then the duty so established will not extend to all cases of wrongful discrimination. Even if, say, gendered dress codes on the job involve wrongful discrimination and treating men and women as having different *social* value, perhaps they do not imply that those of different genders have different *moral* value (see Section 4.3). If the equality at stake in the conclusion is something like social equality, whatever exactly that is, this problem becomes less acute. But the inference is clearly problematic then. Consider a case where, say, bringing about the best outcome on some prioritarian principle involves some people being and being seen as socially slightly inferior, though in a way which they do not mind. Does it follow from the fact that these people have equal moral worth that, in bringing about the relevant outcome, the state violates one of its duties? So much for the assumption that not relating as equals is a wrongful-making feature. We now turn to different ways of relating as unequals.

4.3 Ways of Failing to Treat as Equals

According to Moreau, 'whenever we wrongfully discriminate against others, we fail to treat them as equals' (Moreau 2020, 211), thereby wronging them.

There are three ways in which one can do so. First, one might unfairly subordinate the discriminatee – for example, by either marking out the discriminatee and people like her as inferior to others or by contributing causally to people being marked out in that way. Gendered dress codes suggesting that 'it is a part of a woman's role as a waitress to use her body to gratify men' (Hellman 2008, 42; Moreau 2020, 45) but not suggesting something similar about men's role as waiters counts as subordinating women in both of these ways. It, together with many other social norms, structural accommodations, etcetera, is a tiny constitutive part of and helps bring about a situation involving gender inequalities in power and de facto authority as well as differential consideration and censure (Moreau 2020, 55). Importantly, subordination in Moreau's sense is not just a matter of what agents believe, how they deliberate, or the cultural meaning of their actions. It is also a matter of structural accommodations, such as how we have constructed the public, physical space in a way that it is less well suited to the needs of those who are deviant in a purely statistical sense – for example, disabled people who are unable to access buildings through staircases.

Second, one can fail to treat people as equals by violating their right to deliberative freedom. By this Moreau means real freedom to deliberate about a certain matter without having to take into account the facts that one has or is believed by others to have a certain trait and that others hold certain beliefs about what people with that trait are or should be like. Not all traits involve the right to the corresponding deliberative freedom. If Joe is a serial offender, he has no right to deliberate about whether to commit yet another offense independently of the court's view of serial offenders. However, there are properties – for example, one's gender – where in many contexts one has the right to deliberative freedom. In those cases, violation of someone's deliberative freedom is failing to treat this person as an equal.

Third, one might fail to treat others as equals by depriving them of basic goods. By a 'basic good' Moreau does not mean a good satisfying needs at the lower end of Maslow's pyramid. Rather, she means 'a good access to which is necessary' if one is to be, and is to be seen as, an equal in one's society – for example, the right to marry a person whom you love in a society where marriage is an important institution (Moreau 2020, 249, 126). For this third category to remain distinct from the two previous ones, it presupposes an understanding of what goods are such that not any act or set of acts that subordinates a person or deprives them of their deliberative freedom ipso facto involves depriving them of a basic good.

This classification of three ways of not relating as equals through discrimination is helpful in that it casts a certain interpretative light on different putative cases of subordination. However, there is an inferential step from an account of what makes a general pattern of action morally objectionable to an account of what makes individual acts of discrimination which (causally) 'contribute' to (Moreau 2020, 47, 60), 'confirm' (Moreau 2020, 36), 'express' (Moreau 2020, 48), or 'sustain' (Moreau 2020, 48), etcetera the relevant morally objectionable patterns wrongful (Lippert-Rasmussen 2021, 582–583). Patterns of action contributing to global warming – for example, flying – are morally objectionable. But many think that we cannot infer from that objectionableness that any individual contributory act to global warming is wrongful. Act-consequentialists might argue that my not flying would make my life worse while making no noticeable difference to global warming. Whether this view is sound is not to the point. The point is that there are considerations that can block the inference from a pattern – for example, subordination – being morally objectionable to the individual acts – for example, individual acts of discrimination – that 'contribute to' that pattern being morally wrongful.

Consider next Moreau's specific thoughts on how discrimination is sometimes wrongful because it violates the discriminatee's right to deliberative freedom. Imagine that women and men in one sense have all the same options – for example, members of both genders can become lawyers, officers, etcetera. In another sense they have different options, since any option is proportionally less valuable – say 10 per cent – to women than to men due to sex discrimination. Simplifying: if a male officer earns £100,000, a female officer earns £90,000; if a male lawyer earns £200,000, a female lawyer earns £180,000, etcetera. This difference is irrelevant to women's deliberations about what to do, since *whatever* they do, their options will be proportionally less good than the same options are for men. Unlike ordinary sexist discrimination, which makes a difference to how different options are ranked relative to one another across different genders, this form of sexist discrimination does not. Since it amounts to wrongful discrimination, it represents a challenge insofar as the wrongfulness of this case is not supposed to be captured only in terms of subordination (but see Moreau 2020, 85).

4.4 Social and Moral Equals

According to the relational egalitarian account, discrimination is wrongful because of how it involves not relating to the discriminatees as equals. However, just as one cannot be good full stop, but must be good in some respect, people can be equals only in some respect. There are two obvious candidates here: moral and social status (Lippert-Rasmussen 2024a). Relational egalitarians typically point to moral equality as the foundation of relational egalitarianism. Christian Schemmel (2021, 3) observes approvingly: 'Hardly anybody denies that people are fundamentally each other's moral equals; and not many deny that this basic equality grounds a claim to stand ... as a social and political equal.' Schemmel's idea is that one must relate to others in a way that expresses what they are – that is, moral equals (cf. Hellman 2008, 30) – and that certain forms of social and political relations do not do that. There is an important distinction here. It is one thing to act in a way which expresses that one is not an equal and another not to act in a way that expresses that one is an equal. Acts of the former kind imply that the other is an inferior or a superior, while acts of the latter do not. The latter kind of acts might not express *anything* about the status of the person in question.

With this distinction in place, we can now eye a challenge to the relational account. Many acts that relational egalitarians condemn do not express anything about the moral status of the individuals involved, and to the extent that they do, they do not express that the individuals in question have a lower (or higher) moral status. Take the dated idea that men should hold doors for women. Presumably, this practice expresses something about the relation between men and women that relational egalitarians want to object to – for example, that men are supposed to assist women while women are supposed to gratefully receive unnecessary male assistance. However, it is unclear that this distorted view expresses that women have a lower *moral* status than men. Certainly, the practice does not express – not when considered on its own, at any rate – that the interests of women count for less than those of men. It might express the false view that women need assistance while men do not, but that has nothing to do with moral status. A fortiori, many practices that relational egalitarians want to condemn do not express that any persons have a lower moral status than others. As we have already seen, it is not a general truth that one must act in a way that expresses that a person is what they in fact are. If I act in a way that expressed that a person who is not a grateful person at all is grateful, that is not wrongful. It might be wrongful because of how it leads others to misjudge the character of that person, but if so, then it is not the false expression but rather the consequence of the false expression that is the wrongful-making feature.

This speaks in favour of social status being the respect in terms of which people should relate as equals. If relating as if one has unequal social status is what is objectionable about discrimination, presumably many of the forms of discrimination that are wrongful but, arguably, do not involve relating to discriminatees as if they have an inferior moral status do fall under the relational account – for example, the gendered door holding norms express a social convention to the effect that men are in charge and women are supposed to rely on men's assistance and in this sense are not their *social* equals. However, the flip side of that advantage is a weakness: to wit, that the social world involves many unequal social positions and statuses and that it is implausible that treating people in ways which express those differences amounts to wrongful discrimination across the board. For example, in university seminars the social norm is that, within certain constraints, the teacher gets to decide who speaks when. Treating students and professors differently in a way which reflects their different social positions in this regard arguably is not wrongful.

In sum, relational egalitarians face a dilemma: the norm to which they appeal in their explanation of the wrongness of discrimination states that one must relate to others as either moral or social equals. If the former, then the account is unable to explain the wrongfulness of many cases of intuitively wrongful discrimination that, however, do not involve relating to people as if they have unequal moral status. If the latter, then the account implies that many cases of differential treatment based on justifiable differential social norms amount to wrongful treatment, even wrongful discrimination. There are things to be said in response (Kolodny 2023, 97–101); my point is just that more needs to be said.

4.5 Wrongless Discrimination amongst Unequals and Wrongful Discrimination amongst Equals

There are other reasons to be sceptical of the relational egalitarian account. Like the two previous accounts, the relational egalitarian account is vulnerable to two kinds of objections: cases involving non-wrongful discrimination where people do not treat each other as equals, and cases of wrongful discrimination where the discriminator treats the discriminatee as an equal. The latter kind of counterexample shows that features other than treating as an unequal are wrongful-making features of discrimination. The former casts doubt on whether treating as an unequal is a wrongful-making feature of discrimination.

Starting with the latter and arguably less challenging counterexample, it is natural in light of the two previous sections to scan for cases where, intuitively, discrimination is wrongful because of how it harms or disrespects the discriminatee but does not involve treating the discriminatee as an unequal. A possible example of such a case is an indirectly discriminatory practice involving treating everyone the same, but which for reasons unrelated to ill will, negligence, etcetera imposes disproportionate costs on members of a certain group. Intuitively, such a case might count as wrongful indirect discrimination because of the disproportionate harm involved. Of course, if the practice contributes causally to keeping a historically disadvantaged group at the bottom of society Moreau might say that it subordinates its members and for that reason involves relating to these people as unequals. However, we can simply stipulate that this is not the case. In part, because definitions of indirect discrimination (Section 5.2) do that specify that for something to be an instance of indirect discrimination, it must reproduce social hierarchy of the relevant sort or be part of a set of practices that does. Also, not all consequences of a certain practice bear on whether it is indirectly discriminatory. Hence, because of such consequences that serve to undermine a social hierarchy, it could be the case that a practice is indirectly discriminatory against a certain minority even if, overall, it contributes causally to moving it away from the bottom of society.

What about the other type of counterexample – that is, cases of wrongless discrimination where discriminatees are treated as unequals? Such cases exist. Suppose that, due to some naturally occurring event, an act involving subordination of members of a particular group is required to avoid great harm to these individuals and is performed for that reason. Arguably, these individuals are not treated wrongfully – not even pro tanto – by that act of discrimination.

4.6 Conclusion

This section concludes a series of three sections on what makes discrimination wrongful when it is. These accounts are not the only ones on offer, but arguably they are the three most important. Although they differ in that there are cases of discrimination that will be condemned as wrongful by one of the accounts but not the two others, many instances of wrongful discrimination will be condemned by all three of them. For the purposes of applied political philosophy, it is nice if different accounts of the wrongfulness of discrimination have overlapping implications regarding specific instances of discrimination. However, theoretically it is important to know what accounts for the wrongfulness of discrimination, and, as we have seen, all three accounts seem vulnerable to a range of challenges, either showing that the relevant account cannot stand alone or that the feature which the account in question focuses on is not always a wrongful-making feature of discrimination. To subject our three accounts to further scrutiny, I examine three important kinds of discrimination in the following three sections.

5 Indirect Discrimination

5.1 Introduction

In this and the next two sections, we look at three important forms of discrimination. Doing so serves two purposes. The first purpose is to understand the nature of these kinds of discrimination. Second, through analysing them and why they are wrong, we can identify strengths and weaknesses of our three accounts of what makes discrimination wrong. In this section, we examine the issue of indirect discrimination. Section 5.2 expounds the definition of indirect discrimination. Section 5.3 explores who the victims of indirect discrimination are. Section 5.4 explores the disproportionality condition with an eye to the so-called levelling down objection and to the question of what makes indirect discrimination wrongful. Section 5.5 examines whether the harm-based, the disrespect-based, and the relational accounts of the wrongness of discrimination can account for the wrongfulness of indirect discrimination.

5.2 Defining Indirect Discrimination

According to the definition of indirect discrimination offered in Section 1:

> A discriminator indirectly discriminates against a discriminatee relative to a comparator if, and only if:
>
> (4) the discriminator treats the discriminatee and the comparator in the same way;
> (5) treating the discriminatee and the comparator in this way disadvantages people like the discriminatee relative to people like the comparator; and
> (6) the disadvantages imposed on people like the discriminatee are disproportionate relative to the benefits involved in treating the discriminator and the comparator and people like them in the relevant way.

Condition (4) reflects the general assumption that direct and indirect discrimination are mutually exclusive. Condition (5) specifies that we are discussing indirect discrimination *against*. The disadvantage referred to in (5) is indirect, as it were, because the rule based on which people are being negatively affected neither refers to nor is motivated by their being members of the group they form. Rather it is motivated by some other ground where, however, whether one satisfies the conditions the rule specifies is correlated with whether one belongs to the group in question. Finally, (6) is needed to avoid indirect discrimination being too broad a concept. For virtually any rule, we can identify groups that would be better placed under an alternative one. However, it is not the case that, for virtually any rule, there are groups which are indirectly discriminated against by the practice. By requiring disproportionality, we narrow down the concept of indirect discrimination in a way which prevents it from being omnipresent. So much for the general definition of indirect discrimination.

5.3 Victims of Indirect Discrimination?

Suppose a company promotes employees based on performance on a certain test. The test was adopted because managers in the human resources department reasonably thought that it was the best test available for identifying those who, if promoted, would do best in their new positions. It turns out that, say, white employees generally do better on the test than Hispanic employees. Plausibly, the use of this test disadvantages Hispanic employees relative to using a test which Hispanic employees pass in greater numbers. Suppose, moreover, it is also the case that the benefits to the company of using the test are disproportionately small compared to the disadvantages imposed on its Hispanic employees. Accordingly, the use of the test is indicted on grounds of indirect discrimination. Two questions arise in connection with the question of who the victim of this instance of indirect discrimination is. First, compare the case just described with a similar but reverse case where Hispanics pass the test in greater number than white employees. Is that case one of indirect discrimination too, if the former is? Second, in the original case, who exactly are the Hispanics who were treated wrongfully by indirect discrimination?

In relation to the first question, basically what we are asking is whether, like minority people, majority people can be subjected to indirect discrimination. The answer to this question depends how exactly one distinguishes majority from minority groups – for example, is such identification based on historical facts or only facts about the present situation? Here I shall set this question aside, simply noting that some theorists would say that, unlike direct discrimination, which is symmetric, indirect discrimination is asymmetric in that only people belonging to minority groups can be subjected to it (see Laborde 2024). Hence, in the reverse case, white employees would not be subjected to indirect discrimination even if their Hispanic colleagues are. Theorists who think that indirect discrimination is symmetric might agree, say, that, generally, indirect discrimination against minority groups is worse than otherwise comparable indirect discrimination against majority people – for example, non-promoted white employees might have better opportunities for advancement in other companies than non-promoted Hispanic employees. In the context of US legal theory, the issue of whether discrimination is symmetric has been an ongoing issue for years, where so-called anticlassificationists argue that the point of discrimination law is to prevent citizens from being treated disadvantageously based on certain protected traits, whereas so-called antisubordination theorists argue that its point is to eliminate caste-like social hierarchies between different groups of citizens. The former thinks discrimination law is or ought to be symmetric, whereas the latter think it is or ought to be asymmetric, protecting only minorities (Fiss 1976).

In relation to the second question – who exactly are the Hispanics who were treated wrongfully by indirect discrimination? – there are at least three views to consider. One view is that it is the company's Hispanic employees only, or perhaps a subset of them – that is, those who apply for promotion or would apply for promotion if the test being used by the company were different. Another view is that Hispanics in general are the victims of the indirectly discriminatory use of the test. This view might seem particularly appealing if Hispanics are generally disadvantaged and if the disadvantages that the test involves for them are either causally related to the determinants of their general disadvantage or involve obstacles for Hispanics that they typically encounter on the labour market. The third and more complex view conjoins the two former views and says that while the company's Hispanic employees are the immediate victims of the indirectly discriminatory test, Hispanics in general are also victims of the indirectly discriminatory test.

It is important which of these views we embrace. Eidelson, for instance, seems to adopt the second view and infers that indirect discrimination is not really a form of discrimination. In his view, indirect discrimination law should be thought of not primarily as a matter of preventing discrimination, but more like a means of promoting certain, often laudable goals regarding redistribution across different groups in society (Eidelson 2015, 51; Gardner 1996, 365). Which view should we adopt?

On the first view, it is dubious whether we should be concerned about indirect discrimination. Suppose, counterfactually, that Hispanics in general are neither disadvantaged by the specific use of the test, nor are they generally disadvantaged on the job market, and that there is no systematicity across different companies regarding which groups pass the promotion test in lower numbers. In that case, plausibly, the use of the relevant test does not wrong Hispanic employees. We do not in general assess all sorts of practices within companies regarding whether they harm different groups, however delimited, to an equal degree. This suggests that the connection to wider disadvantage – not just for the specific employees in question, but for the wider socially salient groups of which they are members – is crucial for the purpose of identifying the victims of wrongful indirect discrimination.

Consider the second view – that is, the view that Hispanics in general are the victims of the indirectly discriminatory test. This view avoids the previous challenge. However, it faces another, which is that the test in question might not disadvantage Hispanics in general. It is even possible that the use of the test in question (or, more plausibly, the use of tests like the one in question by companies in general) benefits Hispanics in general. But if that is so, our definition of what counts as indirect discrimination does not align well with a central moral concern underpinning the opposition to indirect discrimination. If the use of the test in question promotes the position of an unjustly disadvantaged group, it is unclear that this is not a morally weightier reason in favour of using the test than the moral reason to eliminate the disadvantage imposed by its use on a tiny subset of Hispanic employees of a specific company. The point here is not that it is particularly likely that a practice by a certain company that disadvantages its employees from a certain group at the same time also benefits members of that group in general. The point is to query where our moral concern with indirect discrimination is located, in a possible case where this mismatch arises. My contention is that in such a case our moral concern should lie with the wider group of individuals. The upshot is that, in the case I imagine, Hispanic employees would not be subjected to wrongful indirect discrimination. However, that view is revisionary in the sense that many probably would consider the case indirectly discriminatory against Hispanic employees.

In short, indirect discrimination theorists can adopt a narrow view on who the victims of indirect discrimination are. In that case, it is unclear why indirect discrimination amounts to wrongful treatment. Alternatively, they can adopt a broad view according to which the victims are the socially salient groups of which the victims of indirect discrimination are members. In that case, they should adopt a revisionary view of what counts as indirect discrimination. Perhaps this is the right way to go, but they will then mean something different by 'indirect discrimination' than what folks have in mind. There is a third option – that is, the complex, conjoint view. However, instead of solving the problems facing the two views that it conjoins, this view seems to inherit the problems of its constituent views.

5.4 Disproportionality

What makes indirect discrimination wrongful? If we look at the definitional elements of indirect discrimination, clearly (4) – that discriminator treats different people in the same way – is not what makes indirect discrimination wrong. Definition (5) – that indirect discrimination disadvantages the discriminatee – is relevant, but its significance seems captured by (6) – that is, that the harm to discriminatees caused by the putatively indirectly discriminatory policy is disproportionate relative to the benefits caused by the putatively indirectly discriminatory policy. This gives rise to a pressing question regarding when disadvantages are disproportionate relative to the benefits. Here I want to focus on three such issues.

First, there is a general issue regarding whether all benefits and harms causally downstream from the indirectly discriminatory act count for the purpose of assessing disproportionality. This is an issue which is like, say, the issue of whether all benefits and harm causally downstream from a certain priority setting in healthcare matter for its moral justifiability. Here many say that only certain kinds of harms and benefits matter – for example, health-related harms and benefits and only relatively direct effects. If we are (un)attracted to such a view in a healthcare setting, we should probably be (un)attracted to a similarly restrictive view in the context of indirect discrimination.

Second, we need to determine what it is for the relevant harms and benefits to be related in a way that involves disproportionality. Is it sufficient for the disadvantage to indirect discriminatees to be greater than the corresponding benefits to others, or must it be significantly greater? There are two ways to understand the disproportionality condition here: moralised or non-moralised.

On a moralised understanding, whether a certain disadvantage is disproportionate entails something about its moral qualities, whereas on a non-moralised understanding this is not the case. On a simple moralised analysis, a disadvantage is morally disproportionate relative to the corresponding benefits if, considering the relationship between the two, it is morally unjustified to impose it. On this interpretation, if a disadvantage is disproportionate, by definition, it is morally wrong to impose it on the victims of indirect discrimination. On a very straightforward non-moralised analysis, a disadvantage to the victims of indirect discrimination is disproportionate if the harm which falls on them is greater than the advantages the discrimination gives to others. On this view, it does not follow from the fact that a disadvantage is disproportionate that it is morally unjustified to impose it. Where the disadvantage *is* unjustified, that is so not because indirect discrimination has occurred, but because some independent moral principle has been infringed.

Neither understanding of proportionality is unproblematic. If we embrace the moralised conception, we cannot say that a policy is made morally wrong by being indirectly discriminatory. Rather, one reason that policy *is* indirect discrimination is that it is morally wrong. By way of analogy consider 'murder'. Murder is a moralised concept in that, by definition, it is a morally wrongful type of killing. But even if something's being murder entails that it is morally wrongful, what *makes* it morally wrongful cannot be that it is murder. Rather, part of what makes an action murder is that it is morally wrongful (Ishida 2021). However, many discrimination theorists think that the fact that something is indirect discrimination *makes* it wrong. Hence they must opt for the non-moralised view.

On the non-moralised view, however, discrimination simply falls out of the picture. It is the fact that indirect discrimination involves the imposition of disproportionate disadvantages on a group of people that makes it wrong. However, there is no reason to think the wrongness of such an imposition is tied narrowly to indirect discrimination, since it could also arise in connection with harms to members of a socially non-salient group. Moreover, it is likely to be unclear that this kind of disadvantage imposition is wrong in general. Indirect discriminators typically adopt all sorts of policies – for example, about where to build factories, what sort of research to invest in, and which goods to produce – that benefit some people and harm others (Hellman 2018, 108). These policies could be assessed in terms of disproportionality. However, few believe that they should be so assessed applying the standards of proportionality used in typical indirect discrimination cases. Judging by their behaviour, most people think it is permissible to make decisions about how to spend one's money which are strongly disproportionate in the sense that they involve tiny benefits for themselves (e.g., dining at a fancy restaurant) and not preventing much greater harms to others (e.g., by providing them with medicine through a donation to Oxfam). But if indirect discrimination is morally wrong because of its disproportionality, so must decisions about where to build factories be. Indeed, in relation to a great deal of decisions, many would say that it is the relevant agent's prerogative to select an option that is disproportionately harmful according to the standards of proportionality used in typical indirect discrimination cases.

Can we say that this shows that many more decisions are wrong because they are indirectly discriminatory than we suppose? That might be a sensible response for those who think indirect discrimination names a particular wrongful action. After all, it is hard to see why, say, hiring policies could be pro tanto morally wrong in virtue of their disparate effects on minorities, whereas otherwise relevantly similar investment policies with similar disparate effects are not. However, many will be reluctant to go down this route given the radical expansion of policies which potentially could then amount to wrongful indirect discrimination. They might instead respond to the present line of argument by rejecting the view that indirect discrimination is non-instrumentally wrong. They will then have to explain why, for example, for pragmatic reasons connected with the successful operation of the law, we have reason to treat indirectly discriminatory hiring decisions differently from many other decisions resulting in disproportionate disadvantage (Steuwer and Lippert-Rasmussen 2024).

The third issue pertains to how to understand the nature of the disadvantages which factor into proportionality assessment. If a disadvantage is disproportionate, it is disproportionate relative to something else. But what, exactly, is the thing we are to compare the discriminatees' disadvantage with to determine whether its imposition is disproportionate? Call this the issue of the proper comparanda. There are two views here, the first one of which is the one most common:

> *The Group Comparison View*: A group of indirect discriminatees is disproportionately disadvantaged by a policy if, and only if, the inequality between that group and a comparator group is greater with the policy than it would be in some relevant alternative situation without the policy.

The Advantages Comparison View: A group of indirect discriminatees is disproportionately disadvantaged by a policy if, and only if, the gap between the advantages it would enjoy under that policy relative to the greater advantages that it would enjoy under some relevant alternative policy is disproportionate relative to the gap between the advantages some comparator group would enjoy under that policy relative to the smaller advantages the comparator group would enjoy in some relevant alternative situation without it (Lippert-Rasmussen 2015, 2022).

To see how these two views differ, consider a situation where we must choose between two policies, Equal and More. Both men and women will be best off under More, but it involves inequality in men's favour. Under Equal, there will be equality between men and women, but both groups will be worse off than they would have been under More. Here, the Group Comparison View implies that women are disproportionately disadvantaged by More – the inequality between men and women is greater under More than under Equal. The Advantages Comparison View need not have this implication, because neither men nor women are disadvantaged under More in comparison with Equal.

On the whole, those alleging indirect discrimination do not distinguish between Group Comparison and Advantages Comparison. If they do, they are likely to assume that, in practice, a policy that is disproportionate in one sense will be so in the other as well. But as More and Equal show, this assumption could be false. Accordingly, to say whether indirect discrimination is non-instrumentally wrong, we need to consider both explications of the comparanda of disproportionality. There are troubles ahead whichever view we take.

Consider, first, the Group Comparison View. On this view, unless you subscribe to distributive egalitarianism in a group-focused version, you cannot regard indirect discrimination as non-instrumentally wrong. But many justice theorists reject distributive egalitarianism in light of the so-called levelling down objection. That objection asks us to consider a situation of equality in which no one is better off in any respect than they would have been in an alternative situation without equality, and then invites us to agree that the equal situation is in no way better than the latter unequal situation (Parfit 1998). People who are impressed with the levelling down objection yet started out with egalitarian sympathies typically switch allegiance to prioritarianism (Arneson 2022; Holtug 2010). But in the prioritarian perspective, a policy that is indirectly discriminatory, if the disproportionality condition is interpreted in terms of the Group Comparison View, might be one that brings about the best outcome and thus is not non-instrumentally wrong. Even on a strict egalitarian view, disproportionality as presently understood need not be a non-instrumentally wrong-making feature. This is so because the currency of the disadvantages involved in the relevantly indirectly discriminatory rule (e.g., proportion of women employees) typically is not the currency of egalitarian justice (e.g., access to advantage) (Cohen 2011).

The Advantages Comparison View avoids this problem, but it creates another: the problem of revisionism. Some cases that most of us would consider to be clear instances of indirect discrimination do not satisfy the disproportionality condition so interpreted. Consider Khaitan's (2018, 31) description of indirect discrimination as 'an apparently neutral practice or policy which puts members of a protected group (say, women) at a disproportionate disadvantage compared with members of a cognate group (say, men)'. The idea here is that, roughly, we can simply compare the proportion of, say, male to female employees to determine whether indirect discrimination has taken place. 'Roughly' because the differential representation must somehow result from the policies (practices, acts, etc.) of the indirectly discriminating agent and be disproportionate relative to the benefit obtained through the policy (Khaitan 2018, 41). However, on the Advantages Comparison View it is possible for a policy to result in, say, a greater proportion of male (or female) employees even if it is not indirectly discriminatory. On this view, indirect discrimination might be non-instrumentally wrong even if we reject distributive egalitarianism, but only if we think differently about the conditions under which a policy is indirectly discriminatory and reclassify various seemingly clear-cut cases of indirect discrimination as cases that are free of that form of discrimination. While the notion of 'disproportionality' is often used without much explanation, it really introduces a wide range of complex issues (see also Section 7.6).

5.5 Indirect Discrimination, Harm, Disrespect, and Inequality

It is time to return to the three accounts of the wrongfulness of discrimination from Sections 2 to 4. Offhand, a harm-based account seems better placed to explain the wrongfulness of indirect discrimination. By definition, indirect discrimination focuses on (disproportionate) harms. Moreover, insofar as disrespect is tied to objectionable mental states, it is unclear that indirect discrimination must be disrespectful given that, arguably, indirect discrimination does not involve objectionable and thus potentially disrespectful mental states. Finally, precisely because indirect discrimination involves treating discriminatees no differently from non-discriminatees, it might seem unclear that indirect discrimination violates relational equality. Hence, insofar as we find indirect discrimination to be wrongful to its discriminatees, it seems we will have to accept that the harm-based account captures at least part of the truth about what makes discrimination wrongful. However, appearances are deceptively simple. There are at least three reasons why.

First, if the disproportionate disadvantages involved in discrimination are comparative across groups and if the harms at stake in harm-based accounts of the wrongfulness of discrimination are comparative across the actual state of affairs and a counterfactual state of affairs where the discriminatory act did not take place, the fact that indirect discrimination disproportionately harms discriminatees does not entail that these discriminatees are harmed in a sense that matters for the purpose of a harm-based account of discrimination. Hence, if we adopt the Group Comparison View (Section 5.4), we cannot at the same time appeal to the harm-based account to explain what makes indirect discrimination wrongful.

Second, as we have seen, not all disrespect-based accounts are tied to the presence of objectionable mental states. Hellman's objective meaning account is compatible with indirect discrimination being demeaning. Presumably, the cultural meaning of facially neutral rules adopted for non-biased reasons could be demeaning – for example, in the light of the fact that women's underrepresentation in parliaments has been seen as a gender issue for many years and yet persists might result in the cultural meaning of such underrepresentation itself being demeaning of women despite the (hypothetical) absence of any direct discrimination against female politicians. However, one might suspect that it is more likely that it is the relevant disproportionate pattern of promotion, say, that is demeaning as opposed to the rules generating that disproportionate pattern. Moreover, on Eidelson's account, if the reason that an indirect discriminator does not change a practice imposing disproportionate disadvantages on discriminatees is a failure to properly attend to the discriminatees' interests, then such discrimination will qualify as disrespectful on Eidelson's account.

Finally, while it might be difficult to see how an individual instance of discrimination violates a norm of relating as equals, relational egalitarians can object to at least systematic forms of indirect discrimination on grounds of relational inequality. Certainly, indirect discrimination systematically disadvantaging a specific group can contribute to subordination of the group in Moreau's sense, loss of deliberative freedom, and lack of access to socially necessary goods.

5.6 Conclusion

In this section, we have seen that indirect discrimination is a complex concept and that it is both unclear who the relevant victims of wrongful discrimination are, and what disproportionate disadvantage amounts to. We have also examined the wrongfulness of indirect discrimination in relation to the three accounts of wrongful discrimination presented in Sections 2 to 4. The harm-based account might seem better placed to account for it, but the picture that emerged was blurred.

6 Implicit Bias Discrimination

6.1 Introduction

The early discrimination literature focused on discrimination based on explicit biases. Paradigm cases of discrimination were cases where, say, a racist employer refuses to hire racial minority applicants because of the employer's belief that members of the relevant racial minority have a lower moral status, or cases such as the opening example of male-only voting rights, where due to sexist ideology women were denied the right to vote. Much of the more recent discrimination literature focuses on implicit bias discrimination. One motivation for this shift is that racist and sexist ideologies have become less widespread. Hence one would expect there to be fewer cases of discrimination based on explicit bias. Even so, many of the distributive gender and racial inequalities persist (Brownstein and Saul 2016, 1). This motivates the hypothesis that discrimination persists, though its primary manifestation is now implicit bias.

Another motivation for the shift in focus from explicit to implicit bias is a series of striking experiments seemingly documenting implicit racial bias even amongst subjects who disavow their biases once made aware of them. The so-called Implicit Association Test (IAT) (see Section 6.2) suggests that, generally, respondents – even many Black respondents – are more disposed to associate various positive features with being white than with being Black (Greenwald, McGhee, and Schwartz 1998). Many take the results of the IAT to suggest widespread implicit bias against African-Americans (Brownstein 2019; Nosek et al. 2007; see also Greenwald and Banaji 1995). Though it is contentious what exactly, if anything, we can learn with regard to discrimination from the IAT, there is little doubt that the IAT has significantly transformed the literature on discrimination.

In this section, I take a closer look at what implicit bias is and how it is different from explicit bias (Section 6.2). Section 6.3 examines whether implicit biases, and actions resulting from them, are morally wrongful. Section 6.4 examines the connection between implicit bias and discriminatory actions. Presumably, dispositions to form particular associations are not actions and, thus, if only actions can be wrong, implicit bias might not be wrongfully discriminatory as such. The question then is whether implicit biases result in wrongful discriminatory actions and what can be done about it. Section 6.5 examines whether agents are morally responsible for their implicit biases if implicit biases are automatic, subconscious, and beyond their control.

One word of caution: for simplicity, I shall refer to implicit biases as if they were more or less one of a kind, even though results in social psychology suggest that they are quite heterogeneous and can operate relatively independent of one another. This has important implications – for example, it might mean that an intervention targeting one implicit bias has no positive effects on other implicit biases (Holroyd and Sweetman 2016).

6.2 What Is Implicit Bias?

The question of what an implicit bias is splits into two sub-questions: what is bias, and what is an implicit, as opposed to an explicit, bias? The core idea of a bias is easy to grasp. Suppose respondents are asked to guess the height of each of the same one hundred individuals. Presumably, all respondents will make mistakes. However, there are three ways respondents may do so. There might be no particular pattern in the mistakes they make – that is, sometimes their guess is too high, sometimes too low. However, the average of their guesses corresponds to the average height of the one hundred individuals. There might also be a particular pattern in the mistakes respondents make. They might tend to either under- or overestimate the height of the one hundred individuals, thus over- or undershooting the average height. In this case, they are biased. There is a target property – the actual height of the individuals in question – and the respondents' estimates systematically err in a particular direction relative to the norm reflected in the target property (Kelly 2022, 4–7, 63–87).

The same sense of bias is at work in the IAT. Respondents will take varying amounts of time performing the individual tasks. But most will systematically take more time to perform the tasks where they have to associate a picture of an African-American face with the answer 'African-American or good' than when they have to associate the same picture with the answer 'African-American or bad'. This involves a bias in the sense that such a difference conflicts with a norm – whether epistemic or moral – that one should not find the first pairing more surprising than the latter, and that the best explanation of why it takes longer to process the first pairing ('African-American or good') than the latter ('African-American or bad') is that processing unexpected associations is more time-consuming; just as one probably would be faster processing 'salt or sugar' – an expected pairing – than 'salt or psychopathy' – an unexpected pairing.

What does it mean for a bias to be implicit? There are at least three related but nevertheless distinct aspects to a bias being implicit (Holroyd, Scaife, and Stafford 2017). First, it is *automatic* in the sense that it is a bias that works independently of deliberation and outside the agent's control and thus is not something that a respondent can simply choose to turn off and thereby successfully inhibit. One way of fleshing this out is through Tamar Gendler's notion of an *alief*: 'to a reasonable approximation, to have an innate or habitual propensity to respond to an apparent stimulus in a particular way. It is to be in a mental state that is ... *a*ssociative, *a*utomatic and *a*rational. As a class, aliefs are states that we share with non-human *a*nimals; they are developmentally and conceptually *a*ntecedent to other cognitive attitudes that the creature may go on to develop. Typically, they are also *a*ffect-laden and *a*ction-generating' (Gendler 2008, 557). Aliefs might, so Gendler conjectures, underpin many implicit biases.

Second, implicit bias is *subconscious* in the sense that typically bearers of implicit biases are unaware of their implicit biases. Implicit biases do not come with any phenomenological qualities, often do not involve propositional content, and their workings are not introspectable (though see Brownstein and Madva 2012a, 2012b; Levy 2015). This does not rule out that once one takes a psychological test and learns that one has an implicit bias, one might know that one has one and even take steps to counteract it.

Finally, bearers of implicit biases do not *identify* with their biases. Unlike the employer who identifies with sexist ideology, bearers of implicit biases are often dismayed to learn of their psychological dispositions, and perhaps the most disturbing result of implicit bias research is that many people who disavow discriminatory attitudes are implicitly biased. Admittedly, a bias could be automatic, subconscious, and also one that the bearer identifies with. However, for simplicity I focus on the form of implicit bias with all three properties (cf. Berndt Rasmussen 2020; Greenwald and Banaji 1995). The relevantly contrasting explicit bias, then, is one which is non-automatic, conscious, and one which the bearer identifies with. This leaves room for intermediate forms of bias, but those I set aside.

6.3 The Wrongfulness of Implicit Bias

The existence of automatic, subconscious, and non-endorsed biases gives rise to at least two questions about moral wrongness. First, is it morally wrong for an agent to be a bearer of such biases? Second, are actions resulting from implicit biases morally wrong? These two questions are related, though distinct. Consider an imaginary agent who is implicitly biased but who is capable of always counteracting their implicit bias. Such an agent might never engage in the sort of discriminatory actions that implicit bias, if unchecked, would result in. Admittedly, studies 'report relationships between implicit bias and behavior in a huge variety of social contexts, from hiring to policing to medicine to teaching and more' (Brownstein 2019). However, the insulation of action from implicit biases is, while psychologically unrealistic, conceptually possible, and this suffices for the relevance of the question as to whether such biases in themselves – that is, independently of their manifestation in actions other than pure mental states (or actions) – are morally wrong.

Let us address the question of the wrongness of implicit bias from the perspective of the three accounts of what makes discrimination wrong surveyed in Sections 2–4. If we start with harm-based accounts, the central question to ask in relation to insulated implicit biases is whether they harm anyone. The answer is that they could, but that it is unlikely that such harms will be great and, if they exist, they will be quite different from the sort of harms that folks typically think make discrimination wrongful insofar as harm makes discrimination wrong when it is. The fact that I have an implicit bias might harm someone who has a preference against my being implicitly biased. If I could school myself out of it at little cost, perhaps that harm makes it wrongful of me not to do so. Still, what this shows is at most that my failure to school myself out of my implicit bias is wrongful, not that my being implicitly biased is itself wrong. Arguably, being implicitly biased does not have the agential nature it must have for it to be something that can be wrong or right in the first place. Just as we do not wrong people whom, in our dreams, we subject to humiliating treatment, because our dreams are something that happen to us and not something we do, we do not wrong anyone by being implicitly biased. Implicit bias being automatic and unconscious means that an agent who in a particular moment manifests an implicit bias is not confronted with two options: one of manifesting the implicit bias – for example, by making a particular association in his mind – and one of not manifesting it. These are two different courses of events, but which of them is actualised is not dependent on the biased person's (present) agency. Perhaps at a previous point in time the agent could have acted otherwise, such that now she would no longer have had the relevant implicit bias, but, again, this might mean that she acted wrongly when not embarking on that debiasing programme in the past. Additionally, because implicit biases are unendorsed and in many ways inaccessible to the agent, arguably, rather than being attributable to the agent, typically they are things that afflict the agent (Levy 2017, 7, 22).

If we shift the focus from implicit biases themselves to actions resulting from implicit biases, the harm-based account seems better placed to explain the wrongness of such actions. To the extent that such actions have harmful effects, not just collectively but individually, the harm-based account can explain why such actions are wrong. Admittedly, many individual actions based on implicit biases might not involve any marginal harms even if they belong to a set of implicitly biased actions that together have very harmful effects. This brings us back to some of the problems discussed in Section 2.3, and has led some authors to think of the moral problem of implicit bias primarily in terms of institutional or structural injustice or discrimination (Anderson 2010; Haslanger 2015).

Consider next the disrespect-based account. Do I disrespect someone if I am implicitly biased against this person – for example, if the first thing that pops up in an employer's mind when they see her at a job interview is the question of whether she will apply for parental leave in the next five years, whereas no such question occurs to the employer in the case of male applicants? Interestingly, Eidelson's deliberation-focused and Hellman's objective-meaning accounts of disrespect might differ here. The objective meaning of someone's manifesting, or even having, implicit bias of the sort just exemplified can be demeaning in Hellman's sense. Accordingly, gender-differentiated patterns of attention can be demeaning even if, in a sense, this fact about the employer's gender-specific pattern of attention is not something they *do* (though perhaps their failing to monitor and resist their differential patterns of attention has an agential character). On Eidelson's (2015, 107–110) account it is less clear that this employer necessarily is disrespectful towards women, though his account accommodates many instances of differential treatment rooted in implicit bias. At least, it could be the case that relative to the information the employer attends to, they respond to the interests of men and women as perceived by them in the same way. It is just that because of implicit bias they perceive facts about men and women's interests differently, or are differentially alert to relevant competing interests depending on the applicant's gender. Perhaps this involves failing to recognise the equal moral standing of women as Eidelson understands the notion, but it is difficult to tell.

Consider finally the relational egalitarian account. No doubt, widespread forms of implicit bias-based discrimination can amount to an important form of social inequality. To the extent that relating as equals has an attitudinal component – that is, that people regard each other as equals – it might even be the case that the mere fact that many people are implicitly biased against, say, disabled people might amount to their not relating to them as equals, even if they never act on those implicit biases. In a sense this seems right, in that to regard someone in a particular way is not something that is under one's immediate agential control; for example, I cannot simply will myself to regard a miser as generous and then do so in virtue of so willing. To the extent that one discriminates on the basis of implicit biases, if anything, that will strengthen the objections of friends of the social equality account. I conclude that our three accounts of what makes discrimination wrongful differ in their implications when it comes to implicit bias discrimination, and that at least on some of them it can be wrongful.

6.4 Mitigation

If implicit bias discrimination can be wrongful or at least have harmful consequences, presumably we want to school people (ourselves included) out of their implicit biases. How can we do that? One suggestion is that we should make people aware of their implicit biases and then feed them information in light of which they can see that their implicit biases are unjustified. Basically, this model assumes that we can mitigate or eliminate implicit biases in the same way that we can prevent epistemically rational agents from holding false beliefs. However, several theorists have expressed scepticism about the viability of this rationalistic approach. On Gendler's view, while beliefs update when the agent acquires conflicting information, paradigmatic aliefs typically do not. Hence, to the extent that aliefs underpin implicit biases, we cannot expect new information to mitigate implicit biases (but see Brownstein and Madva 2012a, 2012b; Madva and Brownstein 2018). Other theorists think that implicit biases cannot be analysed in terms of the notion of alief. Neil Levy (2015), for instance, thinks that implicit biases form a sui generis mental category – patchy endorsements – intermediate between beliefs and mere dispositions to form certain associations. However, he shares the view that implicit biases are deficiently sensitive to new information.

Another suggestion is that implicit biases can be mitigated by manipulating the non-rational processes that generate them in the first place. One approach in social psychology conceives of bias as something that is affected by the degree to which the bearers have contact with the objects of their bias. Not all forms of contact reduce bias, but according to the so-called contact theory, under certain circumstances – for example, equal-status interaction not marked by conflict – contact reduces bias. The contact theory, however, is controversial, and a competing school of thought takes a more pessimistic view, emphasising how increased contact increases awareness of potential conflict and thus, to the extent that conflict underpins biases, potentially the biases themselves.

A third approach emphasises how agents, once aware of their implicit biases, can form conditional implementation intentions to act in ways to counteract their implicit biases. For instance, employers can also be presented with statistics regarding implicit bias in hiring processes and form intentions to take certain precautionary steps counteracting potential implicit gender biases in how they recruit to mitigate their effects – for example, to ask certain questions and not others when they review applications from minority candidates. Again, the size and permanence of the effects of such techniques is debated, and plausibly, in the short term at least, they will at most counteract implicit biases translating into biased actions and not the biases themselves.

Fourth, philosophers taking a structural approach to implicit bias might emphasise that institutions should adopt policies to change the social environment that, by and large, produces our implicit biases in the first place. Such efforts need not be seen as an alternative to individual efforts (Madva 2016). Indeed, widespread support for institutional interventions might be boosted by individuals attending to their own and their peers' biases.

A final and remedial approach is simply to acknowledge that we are implicitly biased and then try to correct posthoc for our implicit biases. For instance, we might try to measure statistically implicit gender bias in the assessment of applications and then adjust scores that reviewers give applicants to counteract the biases that predictably have influenced their rankings (Jönsson and Sjödahl 2012).

6.5 Responsibility

In paradigmatic cases of explicit bias discrimination, the discriminator is blameworthy for their wrongful action. It is unclear that this is the case when it comes to implicit bias discrimination. Suppose John discriminates against women because of his implicit biases. Is he blameworthy for his action? This question is different from whether his action is wrongful. Actions can be blameworthy even if they are not wrongful. Suppose I spitefully spill the water on the floor when someone asks for a drink. Unbeknownst to me, it is poisoned, and I thereby save this person's life. Arguably, I am blameworthy for what I did, even though, in a sense, I did the right thing. Hence, even if we think that implicit bias discrimination is not wrongful, it might still be that we can be blameworthy for it.

However, there are two forceful arguments for why we cannot be blameworthy for implicit bias discrimination. First, arguably one cannot be responsible for what one is not aware of. In general, if one is blamed for an action – for example, saying something hurtful – one response undermining the blame is that one was unaware that what one said was hurtful and, thus, the hurtful action is not one that is relevantly attributable to oneself (cf. Section 3.5). Admittedly, this view is qualified, but not falsified, by the fact that in some cases one ought to have been aware of one's utterance being hurtful, and perhaps in those cases one is blameworthy for having unknowingly said something hurtful (Sher 2009). Similarly, perhaps one can unknowingly engage in wrongful implicit bias discrimination and be blameworthy for so doing on account of the fact that one ought to have known – for example, one failed to reflect on the possibility of oneself harbouring implicit bias, despite one's knowledge that many people in one's situation harbour implicit bias.

Second, arguably one cannot be responsible for what one does not control. This condition is related to the awareness condition to the extent that it is impossible to control something of which one is unaware. However, it is possible to be aware of something that one does not control. Hence, it might be that the control condition rules out that one is responsible for something which the awareness condition does not rule out that one is responsible for. Nevertheless, just as one generally can dismiss blame for something of which one was unaware, one can dismiss blame for something over which one did not exercise control. The control condition is qualified in the same way as the awareness condition – that is, if one ought to have been in a position where one controlled whether one engaged in implicit bias discrimination – for example, one was offered a combination of an implicit bias test and a debiasing training programme – one can be blamed for doing something even if one does not currently control whether one does it.

Admittedly, what exactly 'control' means here is controversial, and some philosophers believe that dismissing blame on grounds of lack of control is generally taken to imply that the agent does not identify with the action for which they are being blamed. Hence, if that implicature is cancelled – the agent wholeheartedly identifies with the action and would have acted no differently had they controlled whether they did – we would still consider the agent blameworthy (Frankfurt 1987). However, even if this point is correct, it is unclear how it bears on responsibility for implicit bias discrimination, given that implicit bias is unconscious and thus hardly something agents can wholeheartedly identify with, even if they would do so were they aware of their bias.

6.6 Conclusion

In this section, I have characterised implicit bias as automatic, unconscious, and unendorsed by the discriminator. Implicit bias discrimination can be wrongful on at least two of our three main accounts of what makes discrimination wrongful. We can also take some steps to mitigate implicit bias discrimination and be blameworthy for engaging in it even though perhaps implicit bias discriminators are more often than explicit bias discriminators not blameworthy for their wrongful discrimination.

7 Algorithmic Discrimination

7.1 Introduction

As noted, when philosophers started theorising wrongful discrimination, the paradigm case of discrimination was that of a human agent making decisions motivated by racial animus or gender prejudice. With the digital revolution, many have started using computer-generated decision-making systems to generate recommendations that human decision makers then use as input in their own decision-making, or even to generate the decisions themselves (Eubanks 2018). Can algorithmic decisions or recommendations be discriminatory? If so, are they discriminatory for the same reasons as human decisions? Can they, or the use of them, be wrongfully discriminatory? Section 7.2 explains the hopes many initially pinned on algorithmic decision-making systems as a way of reducing wrongful discrimination because computers neither can harbour hostility nor be subject to the cognitive malfunctions – for example, motivated reasoning and implicit bias – that human agents are afflicted with. Section 7.3 asks whether algorithmic discrimination is direct or indirect. Section 7.4 looks at the widely debated use of Correctional Offender Management Profiling for Alternative Sanctions (COMPAS), and two central criteria of algorithmic fairness – calibration and equal error rates – that surfaced in this debate, and Section 7.5 at a third view of algorithmic fairness that has grown out of this debate. Section 7.6 returns to our three main accounts of the wrongfulness of discrimination and explores the extent to which they can account for the wrongfulness of algorithmic discrimination. It also briefly examines the view that algorithmic discrimination is wrongful because of how it compounds prior injustice.

7.2 The Promise of Artificial Intelligence and Some Disappointments

If one's starting point is the paradigm case of direct discrimination by a human agent motivated by animus or prejudice, understandably one would be optimistic when it comes to algorithmic decision-making. Machines do not harbour animus against anyone, nor can they be prejudiced. When you design an algorithmic-based decision-making system, you specify all the processable variables that you deem relevant for a certain decision and how they determine what it is going to be. Setting aside the possibility of computer malfunctioning and machine learning where the algorithm auto-adjusts in light of information regarding correct and incorrect decisions (see the Amazon example later in this section), the algorithm will then produce a decision based on the information entered in exactly the way the designer of the program intended it to do. Despite this, many theorists have come to be sceptical of the idea that algorithms will help us reduce the amount of wrongful discrimination.

A major reason for this scepticism is that the datasets on which computers are trained can be biased. A dataset is biased when the data systematically miss their target (Section 6.2) – that is, that regarding which they are supposed to inform their users. One oft-discussed example is crime statistics. Suppose algorithms use data from police reports to estimate which areas of a city are high-crime areas and thus prioritise patrols in those areas. Suppose that police officers are racially biased. Suppose the reason for bias is police officers' knowledge of crime statistics showing that members of certain racial groups are more likely to be involved in certain kinds of crime. Accordingly, police officers are more inclined to stop and frisk people with this racial identity. Thus, they will more often encounter offenders from this group, affecting which incidents of crime they report. Hence, even if there is no difference when it comes to the true crime rate across different racial groups, algorithmic recommendations, etcetera based on data from police reports will reproduce the biases in police practice. Even if the algorithmic processing of the data is unaffected by prejudice and hostility, the output of the algorithms will reflect and reproduce the biases that went into the production of the dataset which the algorithms were fed.

Another example is an algorithm Amazon started using in 2014 to assess job applicants' resumes with the aim of identifying top talent. However, Amazon later scrapped it once it became clear that the computer program tended to rank male over female applicants. The problem was that 'Amazon's computer models were trained to vet applicants by observing patterns in resumes submitted to the company over a 10-year period. Most came from men, a reflection of male dominance across the tech industry ... In effect, Amazon's system taught itself that male candidates were preferable. It penalized resumes that included the word "women's", as in "women's chess club captain". And it downgraded graduates of two all-women's colleges (www.reuters.com/article/idUSKCN1MK0AG).

7.3 Direct or Indirect Discrimination or Neither?

Suppose that, considering cases such as the two just mentioned, we say that algorithmically based decisions can be discriminatory. An obvious question then arises: are such decisions directly or indirectly discriminatory? Clearly, they need not be directly discriminatory. Recall the definition of direct and indirect discrimination in Section 1.3. According to the definition of the former, algorithmic discrimination is direct discrimination only if the algorithm – or perhaps the user of it – represents the discriminatee as a member of a socially salient group and treats the discriminatee worse on account thereof. However, algorithms need not be fed information on the relevant group membership of the discriminatee and, thus, need not represent the discriminatee in this capacity. But even if it did, it is clear that it cannot in the relevant sense treat the discriminatee disadvantageously because of this group membership – for example, it cannot form the intention to treat the discriminatee disadvantageously because of this person's group membership. Users of algorithmically generated recommendations might be similarly unaware of the group membership of the putative discriminatees and simply intend to apply what they believe are the most reliable predictions or correct recommendations.

Similarly, algorithmic discrimination need not be a form of indirect discrimination. Indirect discrimination involves disproportional disadvantages to the discriminatees. However, using datasets that are biased need not do so. That could even be part of the problem – for example, that alternatives to using datasets that are biased against women because of that very sexism is so costly that the disadvantages imposed on women by using them are proportional, in which case using biased datasets does not satisfy the disproportionality condition in the definition of indirect discrimination.

If instances of algorithmically based decisions seem discriminatory and yet might not satisfy standard definitions of neither direct nor indirect discrimination, we must either conclude that they are not instances of discrimination after all or revise our taxonomy of discrimination. One option is to revise our definitions of either direct or indirect discrimination so that instances of putative algorithmic discrimination fall under either (or both) of the two categories. Another option is to introduce a third category of discrimination which is neither direct nor indirect. Together with Hugo Cosette Lefebvre I have proposed:

> *Non-direct Discrimination*: A discriminator non-directly discriminates against people like a discriminatee relative to comparators if, and only if:
>
> (1) The discriminator treats people like the discriminatee and the comparators differently.
> (2) The discriminator does so based on the use of a feature that is meaningfully linked to being a member of a socially salient group of people to which the discriminate belongs.
> (3) How people are treated should not depend on this feature. (Lefebvre and Lippert-Rasmussen 2025).

Because of (1), non-direct discrimination is different from direct discrimination. Because the definition of non-direct discrimination does not include a condition regarding disproportionate disadvantage, non-direct discrimination is different from indirect discrimination. What exactly non-direct discrimination amounts to depends on the idea of 'meaningfully linked' properties. Basically, the idea is that mere statistical correlation between two traits is insufficient for their being meaningfully linked. Rather, it implies that our understanding of what it means to have one of the traits is tied to having the other trait – for example, in the way that being a 'women's chess club captain' is tied in some way to our understanding of being a woman. Not all forms of objectionable algorithmic discrimination are cases of non-direct discrimination, but as the two features selected from the Amazon case suggest, perhaps some are. In any case, to suggest that, taxonomically speaking, the distinction between direct and indirect discrimination is non-exhaustive and we need a third type – non-direct discrimination – to capture certain instances of algorithmic discrimination, one need not commit oneself to a particular view about whether such instances are wrongful. After all, as explained earlier, the concept of group discrimination is non-moralised.

One feature that speaks in favour of adding something like the category of non-direct discrimination, thus replacing the standard dichotomous direct–indirect discrimination distinction with an alternative tripartite one, is that, independently of the issue of algorithmic discrimination, the standard distinction does not exhaust the logical space of discrimination. Suppose an employer adopts a hiring procedure advantaging minority applicants for affirmative action reasons. Such a procedure cannot be directly discriminatory against minority applicants – they are treated better than majority applicants. Suppose, however, that the way in which the procedure advantages minority applicants far from outweighs the benefits accruing to majority applicants due to the fact that the procedure in question is one which more majority applicants successfully pass. Since everyone is not treated the same, the case does not qualify as an instance of indirect discrimination. However, if the procedure without the minority applicant-favouring bits is indirectly discriminatory, then surely the procedure described here is discriminatory too. Yet according to standard definitions it is neither directly nor indirectly discriminatory. With this point noted, I want to address the most-discussed case of algorithmic discrimination and the two main criteria of algorithmic fairness that stood out in this discussion.

7.4 COMPAS, Calibration, and Equal Error Rates

Some US courts use actuarial recidivism risk prediction instruments in estimating an offender's dangerousness and thus the warranted severity of their punishment (Star 2014). One such risk prediction algorithm, COMPAS, uses information about, among other things, an offender's employment and housing status, personality traits, and criminal record to generate a risk score which the courts use in sentencing. COMPAS is not fed information about the offender's race, as this is a legally protected category. In a renowned *Pro Publica* article, Angwin et al. (2016) suggested that nevertheless COMPAS is unfair because it is racially discriminatory.

The basis for the complaint was COMPAS' error rate disparity across Black and white offenders. Basically, the error rate here is the likelihood that, given that an offender reoffends(/does not reoffend), COMPAS will predict that the offender reoffends(/does not reoffend). More specifically, COMPAS is more likely to misclassify a non-reoffending Black offender as dangerous and more likely to misclassify a reoffending white offender as not being so. Being misclassified as dangerous means unjustifiably longer incarceration, while being misclassified as not dangerous means unjustifiably shorter incarceration.

In response, Northpointe – the company which sells COMPAS to courts – disputed that error rate parity is the right criterion of algorithmic fairness. In its stead, the company posited that algorithms are fair if, and only if, they are well calibrated across groups. This means that if the algorithm makes a certain prediction – for example, that the offender will reoffend – then the likelihood of that prediction turning out to be correct is the same across different groups. If COMPAS ascribes, say, a high-risk score of eight to a given offender, then the likelihood that the offender will reoffend should be the same whether the offender is Black or white. COMPAS is roughly well calibrated. Calibration seems like a plausible fairness criterion. Had it turned out, say, that half as many Black as white offenders with a risk score of eight reoffended, many would have seen this to at least indicate racial discrimination against Black offenders.

How can COMPAS be well calibrated and yet involve racial disparities regarding error rates? As became clear in the ensuing debate in the algorithmic fairness literature, because Black offenders have a higher base rate probability of reoffending than white offenders, COMPAS generates more false positives for the former unless, for some high-risk scores, the level of recidivism probability at which the score is given is higher for Black offenders than it is for white offenders. But this would undermine calibration. For mathematical reasons, except in exceptional circumstances equal error rates and calibration are not jointly satisfiable across groups with different base rate probabilities regarding the target property (Chouldechova 2017). Hence, if violating either criterion amounts to unfair algorithmic discrimination, then in almost all situations we will unavoidably engage in unfair algorithmic discrimination, trading off less unfair disparities in error rates against more unfair miscalibration, or the reverse.

While many theorists have endorsed the view that we face such a dilemma, others have denied it, arguing that either parity of error rates or calibration or both is not a criterion of algorithmic fairness. Robert Long (2021) offers the following argument against the view that equal error rates across groups are necessary for algorithmic fairness:

(4) *No Preference*: When there is group-wise inequality of false positive rates, a higher false positive rate does not give members of a group reason to prefer that they had belonged to a group with a lower false positive rate.
(5) *No Preference, No Complaint*: If inequality of some metric does not give members of some group a reason to prefer that they belonged to another group, then members of this group do not have a procedural fairness complaint grounded in the inequality of that metric.
(6) *No Complaint, No Unfairness*: If no member of a group has a procedural fairness complaint grounded in the inequality of that metric, then group-wise inequality of this metric is not sufficient for procedural unfairness towards members of this group.
(7) *Conclusion*: Group-wise inequality of false positive rates is not sufficient for group-wise procedural unfairness.

No Preference is true in COMPAS. COMPAS would have generated the same risk score and thus the same risk of being the victim of a false positive for any offender had this offender had a different race. If an offender had a different racial identity, facts about this offender's employment and housing status, personality traits, and criminal record would presumably have been no different, since such features are not constitutive of the offender's racial identity. *No Preference, No Complaint* rests on the assumption that procedural fairness complaints are grounded in facts about how a procedure disadvantages the complainant. Finally, *No Complaint, No Unfairness* reflects a plausible, individualistic view about how group-based complaints are constituted by complaints on the part of individual members of the group. Group-based complaints do not live a life of their own independently of complaints of the individual members of the group.

Long's argument is forceful and shows that unequal false positives do not entail the existence of a fairness-based complaint against unequal error rates. What about calibration? In non-algorithmic contexts, calibration is generally not regarded as a necessary condition of the absence of unfair discrimination. Consider audit studies. These studies involve survey experiments in which one independent variable, such as race or gender, is altered to determine the effect of so doing. Experimenters might send out many job applications with accompanying resumes. These will be identical except for the applicant's name, which in half of the applications is a male name, and in the other half a female name. If applicants with male-sounding names get more calls than those with female-sounding names, the audit study will conclude that female applicants are subjected to unfair bias. If there is no difference in call-back rates, it will conclude that there is no unfair gender bias.

One powerful thought underlying this inference is that applicants have a claim that their chances of success are not causally influenced by their gender, race, etcetera. Applicants do not have a claim to be called in for an interview. Other applicants might be better qualified. However, they have a claim that their prospects of being invited for an interview depend on their qualifications, and not their gender or race (cf. Vredenburgh 2022 and Moreau on deliberative freedom Section 4.3). Consider now the following imaginary scenario:

> *Job Market*: There are 500 male and 500 female applicants for a certain position. Because of past sexist discrimination preventing female applicants from acquiring the needed work experience, 180 of the male applicants are qualified, while only 20 female applicants are. Hiring is conducted in a non-algorithmic way – that is, the members of the selection committee look at the applications and use their judgement and informal deliberation to form an opinion about who is and who is not qualified. An audit study concludes that the hiring committee is unbiased, gender-wise. For any hired and any rejected applicant, the same outcome would have occurred had this applicant had a different gender. The hiring committee's assessments are quite accurate, but not perfect. If an applicant, whether male or female, is qualified, there is a 90 per cent chance the committee will deem them to be qualified. If the applicant is unqualified, there is a 90 per cent chance the committee will deem them to be unqualified.

This job market scenario involves a non-algorithmic decision procedure which is miscalibrated, even though an audit study will conclude that it involves no unfair bias. If the hiring committee deems a particular applicant qualified, there is a greater chance that the applicant *is* qualified if the applicant is male (162/194) than if she is female (18/66). However, the hiring procedure involves equal false positive and false negative rates across gender. By stipulation, if an applicant is (un)qualified, then in 90 per cent of those cases, the committee will deem the applicant to be (un)qualified whether the applicant is male or female. This reflects that, by stipulation, gender has no causal influence on whether applicants are deemed qualified. Adjusting the assignment of the scores 'qualified'/'unqualified' to reduce miscalibration would not be a way of counteracting unfair bias. Hence, in non-algorithmic hiring contexts with different base rates across different groups of applicants, miscalibration is insufficient for unfair discrimination. It is unclear why algorithmic contexts should be any different (Lippert-Rasmussen 2024c).

This brings us to the second reason why we might reject the view that calibration is necessary for the absence of unfair algorithmic discrimination. In our job market example, if a male applicant had been female instead, this person's chance of being invited for an interview would have been no greater. Hence, if Long's argument defeats parity of error rates as a necessary criterion of algorithmic fairness, a close cousin to it defeats calibration. Specifically, an argument analogous to Long's that defeats calibration replaces *No Preference* with:

> (4*) *No Preference**: When there is base rate-based lack of calibration, the lack of calibration does not give (unqualified) members of a group reason to prefer that they had belonged to a group where the (expected) percentage of individuals assigned this score ('qualified') who are qualified is lower.

And infers:

> (7*) *Conclusion**: When there is base rate-based lack of calibration, lack of calibration is not sufficient for group-wise procedural unfairness.

from (4*), (5), and (6). In sum, there are strong reasons for believing that neither parity of error rates nor calibration are necessary conditions for algorithmic fairness.

7.5 Matched Groups

If neither equal error rates nor calibration are necessary conditions for the absence of unfair algorithmic discrimination, what then is? One promising suggestion by Fabian Beigang (2023) is equal error rates and calibration *across matched groups*. The concept of matched groups is known from the literature on causal inference. If you want to make an inference regarding the causal effect of some treatment, ideally, you want a randomised controlled trial where you randomly sort a sufficiently large sample of randomly selected subjects into two groups: one that is subjected to the treatment whose effect you want to test, and one that is not subjected to any treatment. The two groups match in the sense that there is a very high chance that they differ in relevant ways only in terms of whether they have been subjected to the treatment.

The gist of Beigang's proposal is that instead of error rate equality being a necessary condition for algorithmic fairness, error rate equality across matched groups is. Similarly, instead of calibration across groups being a necessary condition for algorithmic fairness, calibration across matched groups is. First, consider error rate equality across matched groups with respect to COMPAS. The groups of white and Black offenders compared by *Pro Publica* were not matched, because the base rate probability of Black offenders recidivating is higher than in the case of white offenders. Had *Pro Publica* instead compared matched groups of white and Black offenders, presumably, the likelihood of a recidivating offender being predicted by COMPAS to recidivate would have been the same across the two matching groups of offenders given that the informational input would have been the same for the two groups of offenders. Moreover, had it not been, plausibly, COMPAS would involve unfair racial discrimination in that race in and of itself would influence the risk scores generated by COMPAS. In that case, No Preference in Long's argument would have been false.

Next, consider calibration across matched groups in the job market scenario. In that case, the groups of male and female applicants compared were not matched in that male applicants were more likely to be qualified than female applicants. Thus, to see whether this job market case satisfies predictive parity across matched groups, we must compare a group of men and a group of women which do not differ regarding base rate probability of being qualified. If we do that, since, by stipulation, gender has no causal influence on the assessments, calibration across matched groups is satisfied. Moreover, had it not been, plausibly, this would have shown the committee to be involved in unfair gender discrimination, where gender plausibly causally affected the committee's assessments in a way amounting to unfair discrimination. Hence, No Preference* in Long's modified argument is false.

Error rate equality and calibration across matched groups neither clashes with how we think of absence of unfair discrimination in non-algorithmic contexts, nor with Long's (revised) argument, and, in part for that reason, together they appear to be strong candidates for necessary conditions of algorithmic fairness. Incidentally, under perfect matching conditions, equal error rates across matched groups implies calibration across matched groups and vice versa (Beigang 2023, 185). Hence, the dilemmatic trade-off of less unfair disparities in error rates against more unfair miscalibration (now across matched groups) is a less pressing issue.

7.6 Algorithmic Discrimination, Harm, Disrespect, and Inequality

How do the three main accounts of the wrongness of discrimination apply to algorithmic discrimination? Consider first the harm-based account. Suppose that COMPAS was an instance of wrongful algorithmic discrimination either because of error rate disparities, or because of error rate disparities or miscalibration across matched groups. If so, can that be explained by the harm-based account? It is unclear that it can. First of all, if we are to apply the harm-based account, we would have to identify those who are harmed and benefited by COMPAS. Hardly any of the discussions that followed COMPAS had this focus, suggesting that the harm-based account, at least in its general form, was not the main driver of any complaints against it. It is even unclear who was harmed by COMPAS. The complaint was that COMPAS was racially discriminatory, so this might be taken to suggest that COMPAS was wrongful because it harmed Blacks. However, that was not the complaint of *Pro Publica*. In any case, it is unclear whether the use of COMPAS harmed Blacks as a group. If, for instance, the use of COMPAS resulted in longer periods of incarceration of dangerous offenders and if most crime takes place among people who live in proximity to each other, then, because of US racial segregation in terms of residency, perhaps many Blacks benefited from COMPAS by avoiding becoming victims of crimes that would have occurred in its absence. Perhaps the most promising harm-based account of the wrongfulness of COMPAS submits that COMPAS amounted to wrongful discrimination because of how it harmed Black offenders by imposing a greater risk of unjustifiably long incarceration on them. But the harms in question need to be weighed against the benefits to those who would otherwise have become victims of the offenders' crimes. Perhaps this is not surprising because the harm-based account applied to algorithmic decision-making focuses on the substantive outcomes of these decisions, whereas complaints about unequal error rates or miscalibration are better regarded as complaints about procedural injustice.

Similarly, it is unclear that the relational egalitarian account can explain algorithmic unfairness. First, unfair algorithmic decision-making need not mark anyone out as inferior. Whether an instance of fair or unfair algorithmic discrimination, COMPAS identifies both white and Black offenders as dangerous. Second, it is also unclear that it prevents Blacks from deliberating about anything without taking into account their race, since COMPAS was not fed any information about their race. Finally, while incarceration plausibly involves deprivation of a basic good – that is, freedom of movement – insofar as justified incarceration is consistent with relating as equals, arguably Moreau's third way of not relating as equals does not seem present in cases of potentially unfair algorithmic discrimination.

Consider finally the respect-based account of wrongful discrimination. First, Alexander's account seems clearly irrelevant here. The use of COMPAS was not premised on anyone having lower moral status. Next, on Eidelson's deliberation-focused form of disrespect, if algorithmic decision-making is disrespectful it would have to be because the involved parties are insufficiently attentive either to the interests of those who are the object of the predictions or to their autonomy. Neither need be the case. On the assumption that imposing longer periods of incarceration on dangerous offenders is justified – for example, in light of its crime preventive effects – it is unclear that using COMPAS is disrespectful relative to the interest component. Moreover, while COMPAS makes a prediction based partly on demographic facts – for example, one's level of education – and partly on the basis of information that is in some sense more personal – for example, prior convictions, nothing prevents judges from supplementing the information provided by COMPAS with individualised information obtained in court proceedings and on that basis considering whether there are reasons to believe that the offender will autonomously choose to act in ways that differ from the predictions generated by COMPAS. Hence, on Eidelson's account, error rate disparities or miscalibration across (matched) groups do not imply that the algorithmic decision-making in question is disrespectful.

Regarding Hellman's objective meaning account, it is unclear that the use of COMPAS has (or, at least, had) any shared cultural objective meaning as being demeaning. Such a meaning would have to be grounded in an understanding of some of the mathematical aspects of COMPAS – for example, the difference between parity of error rates and calibration, which many probably lack. Hence, how they would interpret them, and whether they would understand them in the same way once they understood them, is unclear.

Recently, Hellman (2020) has proposed explaining the wrongness of algorithmic discrimination not in terms of its demeaningness, but in terms of how it compounds prior injustice. On that account, we compound an injustice when we take it or its effects as a reason for acting in ways that further disadvantage its victims. Applied to COMPAS, the idea is that the higher recidivism in the case of Black offenders reflects existing racial injustice against Blacks and that because COMPAS takes that higher base-rate probability as a reason for imposing a higher risk of being misclassified as more dangerous, it compounds prior racial injustice.

While this account might seem more promising than the three main accounts that we have examined in this Element, it is also not without its problems. Most importantly, while there is something particularly wrongful about compounding injustice, it is unclear that, ultimately, that injustice lies in taking an injustice as a reason for acting in ways that further disadvantage its victims, assuming that this is what the use of COMPAS involves. Arguably, this intuition is better explained by considerations about disrespect and about how compounding injustice often involves making a situation even further removed from ideal distributive justice (Lippert-Rasmussen 2023b; but see Laborde 2024). Cases where injustice is compounded but where this involves neither disrespect nor a deepening of injustice do not seem unjust. To see this, imagine a situation where the agent who uses COMPAS does so with great regret while aggressively reducing the racial injustices underlying differential base rate recidivism disparities and only with the aim of avoiding the greater evil of more innocent victims of crime. In this case, it is unclear that using COMPAS amounts to unjust compounding of injustice.

7.7 Conclusion

In this section, we have examined algorithmic discrimination focusing on COMPAS. We have seen why, despite its initial promise of steering clear of two important psychological sources of direct discrimination – hostility and bias – (the use of) algorithms can arguably be discriminatory, when the algorithms are trained on biased data sets. Next, we asked whether algorithmic discrimination is direct or indirect and suggested that it need not be either, thus suggesting the need for a tripartite distinction between direct, indirect, and non-direct discrimination instead of the standard dichotomous direct–indirect distinction. Then we examined three views about fair algorithms, concluding that Beigang's criterion of equal error rates and calibration across matched groups is superior to calibration and parity rates across unmatched groups. Finally, we looked at the three main accounts of wrongful discrimination, as well as Hellman's recent compounding injustice account, arguing that none of them seems to provide an ultimately satisfying account of what makes COMPAS an instance of wrongful discrimination. This is not to suggest that COMPAS, or for that matter the other candidate examples of wrongful algorithmic discrimination, are not just that. Perhaps we should trust our intuitions about how many uses of algorithms amount to wrongful algorithmic discrimination even though we do not yet have a good explanation of what makes them instances of wrongful discrimination.

8 Conclusion

We have come to the end of this brief Element on wrongful discrimination. We started out with a definition of discrimination as well as different subspecies of discrimination (Section 1). Next, we looked at three of the most prominent recent accounts of what makes discrimination wrongful: the harm-, the disrespect-, and the social equality-based accounts (Sections 2–4). In relation to all three accounts, we identified powerful challenges. In the three remaining sections, we then examined three different subspecies of discrimination – indirect, implicit bias, and algorithmic discrimination – partly with the aim of saying something specifically about these forms of potentially wrongful discrimination, partly with the aim of assessing the three main accounts. I have argued that all three of them face significant challenges in capturing the putative wrongfulness of these subspecies of discrimination. These limitations come on top of the problems identified for each account in Sections 2–4. Overall, the discussion suggests that a monistic account of the wrongfulness of discrimination has relatively dim prospects when it comes to fitting all of our intuitions regarding wrongful discrimination and, indeed, that some, perhaps all, of the three main accounts are yet to find their most appealing form. What these claims imply is a challenge for another time.

References

Alexander, L., "What makes wrongful discrimination wrong? Biases, preferences, stereotypes, and proxies," *University of Pennsylvania Law Review* 141 (1992), 149–219.

Altman, A., "Discrimination," *Stanford Encyclopedia of Philosophy* (2020). https://plato.stanford.edu/entries/discrimination.

Anderson, E., "Epistemic justice as a virtue of social institutions," *Social Epistemology* 26 (2010), 163–173.

Angwin, J., J. Larson, S. Mattu, and L. Kirchner, "Machine Bias," *Pro Publica* (2016, 23 May). www.propublica.org/article/machine-bias-risk-assessments-in-criminal-sentencing.

Arneson, R. "Egalitarianism and responsibility", *Journal of Ethics* 3 (1999), 225–247.

Arneson, R., "Discrimination and harm." In K. Lippert-Rasmussen (ed.), *Routledge Handbook of the Ethics of Discrimination*, London, Routledge, 2017, 151–163.

Arneson, R., *Prioritarianism*, Cambridge, Cambridge University Press, 2022.

Basu, R., "What we epistemically owe to each other," *Philosophical Studies* 176 (2019a), 915–931.

Basu, R., "The wrongs of racist beliefs," *Philosophical Studies* 176 (2019b), 2497–2515.

Basu, R., "Radical moral encroachment: The moral stakes of racist beliefs," *Philosophical Issues* 29 (2019c), 9–23.

Basu, R., "Morality of belief I," *Philosophy Compass* 18(7) (2023a), 1–10. https://compass.onlinelibrary.wiley.com/doi/epdf/10.1111/phc3.12934.

Basu, R., "Morality of belief II," *Philosophy Compass* 18(7) (2023b), 1–9. https://compass.onlinelibrary.wiley.com/doi/10.1111/phc3.12935.

Basu, R., and M. Schroeder, "Doxastic wronging." In B. Kim and M. McGrath (eds.), *Pragmatic Encroachment in Epistemology*, New York, Routledge, 2018, 158–178.

Beeghly, E., "Discrimination and disrespect." In K. Lippert-Rasmussen (ed.), *Routledge Handbook of the Ethics of Discrimination*, London, Routledge, 2017, 83–96.

Beeghly, E., "Discrimination and the value of lived experience in Sophia Moreau's *Faces of Inequality*," *University of Toronto Law Journal* 73 (2023), 112–132.

Beigang, F., "Reconciling algorithmic fairness criteria," *Philosophy & Public Affairs* 51 (2023), 166–190.

Bengtson, A., and L. Munch, "Consensual discrimination," *Philosophical Quarterly* (2024). https://doi.org/10.1093/pq/pqae039.

Berndt Rasmussen, K., "Harm and discrimination," *Ethical Theory and Moral Practice* 22 (2019), 837–891.

Berndt Rasmussen, K., "Implicit bias and discrimination," *Theoria* 86 (2020), 727–748.

Brownstein, M., "Implicit bias." In *Stanford Encyclopedia of Philosophy* (2019). https://plato.stanford.edu/entries/implicit-bias.

Brownstein, M., and A. Madva, "Ethical automaticity," *Philosophy of the Social Sciences* 42 (2012a), 67–97.

Brownstein, M., and A. Madva, "The normativity of automaticity," *Mind and Language* 27 (2012b), 410–434.

Brownstein, M., and J. Saul, *Implicit Bias & Philosophy*, vol. 1, Oxford: Oxford University Press, 2016.

Campbell, C., and D. Smith, "Distinguishing between direct and indirect discrimination," *Modern Law Review* 86 (2023), 307–330.

Cavanagh, M., *Against Equality of Opportunity*, Oxford, Clarendon Press, 2002.

Chouldechova, A., "Fair prediction with disparate impact: A study of bias in recidivism prediction instruments," *Big Data* 5 (2017), 153–163.

Cohen, G. A., *On the Currency of Egalitarian Justice and Other Essays in Political Philosophy*, Princeton, NJ, Princeton University Press, 2011.

Cornell, N., "Wrongs, rights, and third parties," *Philosophy & Public Affairs* 43 (2015), 109–143.

Cosette-Lefebvre, H., "Direct and indirect discrimination: A defense of the disparate impact model," *Public Affairs Quarterly* 34 (2020), 340–367.

Cossette-Lefebvre, H., and Lippert-Rasmussen, K., Neither direct, nor indirect: Understanding proxy-based algorithmic discrimination. *Journal of Ethics* (2025), 1–27.

Crenshaw, K., "Demarginalizing the intersection of race and sex," *University of Chicago Legal Forum* Iss. 1 (1989), 139–167.

Darwall, S., "Two kinds of respect," *Ethics* 88 (1977), 36–49.

Eidelson, B., *Discrimination and Disrespect*, Oxford, Oxford University Press, 2015.

Elster, J., "How outlandish can imaginary cases be?" *Journal of Applied Philosophy* 28 (2011), 241–258.

Eubanks, V. (2018). *Automating Inequality: How High-Tech Tools Profile, Police, and Punish the Poor*, New York, St. Martin's Press.

Fabre, C., "Doxastic wrongs, non-spurious generalizations and particularized beliefs," *Proceedings of Aristotelian Society* 122 (2022), 47–69.

Fiss, O. M., "Groups and the Equal Protection Clause," *Philosophy & Public Affairs* 5 (1976), 107–177.

Frankfurt, H., *The Importance of What We Care About*, New York, Cambridge University Press, 1987.

Fredman, S., "Direct and indirect discrimination: Is there still a divide?" In H. Collins and T. Khaitan (eds.), *Foundations of Indirect Discrimination Law*, Oxford, Hart, 2018, 31–56.

Gardner, J., "Discrimination as injustice," *Oxford Journal of Legal Studies* 16 (1996), 353–367.

Gendler, T., "Alief in action (and reaction)," *Mind and Language* 23 (2008), 552–585.

Greenwald, A., and M. Banaji, "Implicit social cognition: Attitudes, self-esteem, and stereotypes," *Psychological Review* 102 (1995), 4–27.

Greenwald, A., D. McGhee, and J. Schwartz, "Measuring individual differences in implicit cognition," *Journal of Personality and Social Psychology* 74 (1998), 1464–1480.

Haslanger, S., "Distinguished lecture: Social structure, narrative and explanation," *Canadian Journal of Philosophy* 45 (2015), 1–15.

Hellman, D., *When Is Discrimination Wrong?* Cambridge, MA, Harvard University Press, 2008.

Hellman, D., "Indirect discrimination and the duty to avoid compounding injustice." In H. Collins and T. Khaitan (eds.), *Foundations of Indirect Discrimination Law*, Oxford, Hart, 2018, 105–122.

Hellman, D., "Measuring algorithmic fairness," *Virginia Law Review* 106 (2020), 811–866.

Hellman, D., and S. Moreau (eds.), *Philosophical Foundations of Discrimination Law*, New York, Oxford University Press, 2013.

Holroyd, J., R. Scaife, and T. Stafford, "Responsibility for implicit bias," *Philosophy Compass* 12 (2017), 1–13.

Holroyd, J., and J. Sweetman, "The heterogeneity of implicit bias." In M. Brownstein and J. Saul (eds.), *Implicit Bias and Philosophy*, vol. 1, Oxford, Oxford University Press, 2016, 80–103.

Holtug, N., *Persons, Interests, and Justice*. Oxford, Oxford University Press, 2010.

Hosein, A., "Racial profiling and a reasonable sense of inferior political status," *Journal of Political Philosophy* 26 (2018), 1–20.

Ishida, S., "What makes discrimination morally wrong? A harm-based view reconsidered," *Theoria* 87 (2021), 483–499.

Jönsson, M., and J. Sjödahl, "Increasing the veracity of implicitly biased rankings," *Episteme* 14 (2017), 499–517.

Kagan, S., *The Limits of Morality*, Oxford, Clarendon Press, 1989.

Kelly, T. *Bias*, Oxford, Oxford University Press, 2022.

Khaitan, T., *A Theory of Discrimination Law*, Oxford, Oxford University Press, 2015.

Khaitan, T., "Indirect discrimination." In K. Lippert-Rasmussen (ed.), *The Routledge Handbook of the Ethics of Discrimination*, New York, Routledge, 2018, 30–41.

Kolodny, N., *The Pecking Order*, Cambridge, MA, Harvard University Press, 2023.

Laborde, C., "Structural inequality and the protectorate of discrimination law," *Politics, Philosophy & Economics* (2024), 1–24.

Levy, N., "Neither fish nor fowl," *Noûs* 49 (2015), 800–823.

Levy, N., "Implicit bias and moral responsibility," *Philosophy and Phenomenological Research* 94 (2017), 3–26.

Lippert-Rasmussen, K., "'We are all different': Statistical discrimination and the right to be treated as an individual." *Journal of Ethics* 15 (2011), 47–59.

Lippert-Rasmussen, K., *Born Free and Equal? A Philosophical Inquiry into the Nature of Discrimination*, Oxford, Oxford University Press, 2013.

Lippert-Rasmussen, K., "Indirect Discrimination Is Not Necessarily Unjust," *Journal of Practical Ethics* 2 (2015), 33–57.

Lippert-Rasmussen, K., *Relational Egalitarianism*, Cambridge, Cambridge University Press, 2018.

Lippert-Rasmussen, K., "Moreau on discrimination", *Jurisprudence* 12 (2021), 579–590.

Lippert-Rasmussen, K., "Why 'indirect discrimination' is a useful legal but not a useful moral concept," *Erasmus Journal for Philosophy and Economics* 15 (2022), 83–107.

Lippert-Rasmussen, K., "Wrongful discrimination without equal, basic moral status," *Ethical Theory and Moral Practice*, 26 (2023a), 19–36.

Lippert-Rasmussen, K., "Should people who are moral equals relate as social equals? Should people who are not moral equals relate as social equals?" In G. Floris and N. Kirby (eds.) *How Can We Be Equals?* Oxford, Oxford University Press, 2024a, 81–102.

Lippert-Rasmussen, K., "Gated communities and discrimination against the poor." In S. Holmen, J. Ryberg, and T. Søbirk Petersen, *Crime Prevention by Exclusion: Ethical Considerations*, New York, Routledge, 2024b, 142–162.

Lippert-Rasmussen, K., "Algorithmic and non-algorithmic fairness," *Law and Philosophy* (2024c), 1–25.

Lippert-Rasmussen, K., and P. Vallentyne, "Discrimination, Intrinsic Wrongness, and Mental States", *Oxford Studies in Political Philosophy* (forthcoming), 1–18.

Long, R., "Fairness in machine learning: Against false positive rate equality as a measure of fairness," *Journal of Moral Philosophy* 19 (2021), 49–78.

Liu, X., and Y. Liang, "What it means to respect individuality," *Philosophical Studies* 179 (2020), 2579–2598.

Madva, A., "A plea for anti-anti-individualism," *Ergo* 3 (2016), 701–728.

Madva, A., and M. Brownstein, "Stereotypes, prejudice, and the taxonomy of the implicit social mind," *Noûs*, 53 (2018), 611–644.

Mason, A., *What's Wrong with Lookism?* Oxford, Oxford University Press, 2023.

May, S. C., "Directed duties," *Philosophy Compass* 10 (2015), 523–532.

Midtgaard, S. F. and V. Pedersen, "Paternalistic discrimination," *Law and Philosophy* 4 (2024), 235–259.

Mill, John Stuart (1988 [1869]) The Subjection of Women. Indianapolis, IN: Hackett.

Miller, D., *Principles of Social Justice*. Cambridge, MA, Harvard University Press, 2001.

Moreau, S., *Faces of Inequality*, Oxford, Oxford University Press, 2020.

Nosek, B., A. Greenwald, and M. Banaji, "The Implicit Association Test at age 7: A methodological and conceptual review." In J. A. Bargh (ed.), *Automatic Processes in Social Thinking and Behavior*, Philadelphia, PA, Psychology Press, 2007.

Onwuachi-Willig, A. "Reconceptualizing the harms of discrimination: How *Brown v. Board of Education* helped to further white supremacy," *Virginia Law Review* 105 (2019), 343–369.

Parfit, D., *Reasons and Persons*, Oxford: Clarendon Press, 1986.

Parfit, D., "Equality and priority." In A. Mason (ed.), *Ideals of Equality*, Oxford, Basil Blackwell, 1998, 1–20.

Schemmel, C., *Justice and Egalitarian Relations*, Oxford, Oxford University Press, 2021.

Schroeder, M. "When beliefs wrong," *Philosophical Topics* 46 (2018), 115–128.

Segall, S., "What's so bad about discrimination?" *Utilitas* 24.1 (2012), 82–100.

Shelby, T. "Justice, deviance, and the dark ghetto," *Philosophy & Public Affairs* 35 (2007), 126–160.

Sher, G., *Who Hnew? Responsibility without Awareness*. New York, Oxford University Press, 2009.

Sher, G., *The Wild West of the Mind*, Oxford, Oxford University Press, 2022.

Singh, K., and D. Wodak, "Does race best explain racial discrimination?" *Philosophers' Imprint* 23 (2023), 1–22.

Slavny, A., and T. Parr, "Harmless discrimination," *Legal Theory*, 21 (2015), 100–114.

Sorensen, R. A., *Thought Experiments*, New York, Oxford University Press, 1992.

Sreenivasan, G., "Duties and their direction," *Ethics* 120 (2010), 465–494.

Starr, S., "Evidence-based sentencing and the scientific rationalization of deiscrimination," *Stanford Law Review* 66 (2014), 803–872.

Steuwer, B., and K. Lippert-Rasmussen, "The poverty discrimination puzzle," *Political Philosophy* 1 (2024), 293–320.

Tadros, V., "Causal contributions and liability," *Ethics* 128 (2018), 402–431.

Thomas, L., "Statistical badness," *Journal of Social Philosophy* 23 (1992), 30–41.

Thomsen, F. K., "But some groups are more equal than others," *Social Theory and Practice* 39 (2013), 120–146.

Thomsen, F. K., "No disrespect: But that account does not explain what is morally wrong about discrimination," *Journal of Ethics and Social Philosophy*, 23 (2023), 420–447.

Vredenburgh, K., "Fairness." In J. B. Bullock (ed.), *Oxford Handbook of AI Governance*, Oxford, Oxford University Press, 2022. https://doi-org.ez.stats biblioteket.dk/10.1093/oxfordhb/9780197579329.013.8.

Wilkes, K. V. *Real People: Personal Identity without Thought Experiments*, Oxford, Oxford University Press, 1993.

Acknowledgements

I thank Cécile Laborde and two anonymous reviewers for helpful comments and the Danish National Research Foundation (DNRF144) for generous support in relation to this Element.

Cambridge Elements

Political Philosophy

Cécile Laborde
University of Oxford

Cécile Laborde holds the Nuffield Chair in Political Theory at Oxford University. She is the author of *Pluralist Thought and the State* (2000) and *Critical Republicanism* (2008). Her last monograph, *Liberalism's Religion*, was awarded the 2019 Spitz Prize.

Steven Wall
University of Arizona

Steven Wall is Professor of Philosophy at the University of Arizona. He is a founding editor and currently editor of *Oxford Studies in Political Philosophy*. He is the author of *Liberalism, Perfectionism and Restraint* (Cambridge, 1998) and the editor of *The Cambridge Companion to Liberalism* (Cambridge, 2008).

About the series

Cambridge Elements in Political Philosophy offers concise and original introductions to central topics in political philosophy. A broad understanding of the discipline will include discussions of nations, states and communities, global justice, rights, the practice of politics, power and authority, and politics and social life, and new and emerging issues will be covered as well as more traditional problems. Each Element will provide a balanced survey of the current state of debate on the topic in question as well as presenting a distinctive perspective that advances new ideas and arguments.

Cambridge Elements

Political Philosophy

Elements in the Series

Politics and the Economy
Lisa Herzog

Political Meritocracy in the 21st Century
Brian Kogelmann

Wrongful Discrimination
Kasper Lippert-Rasmussen

A full series listing is available at: www.cambridge.org/EPLP

For EU product safety concerns, contact us at Calle de José Abascal, 56–1°, 28003 Madrid, Spain or eugpsr@cambridge.org.

www.ingramcontent.com/pod-product-compliance
Lightning Source LLC
LaVergne TN
LVHW011855060526
838200LV00054B/4338